ALMOST CATHOLIC

An Appreciation of the History, Practice, and Mystery of Ancient Faith

JON M. SWEENEY

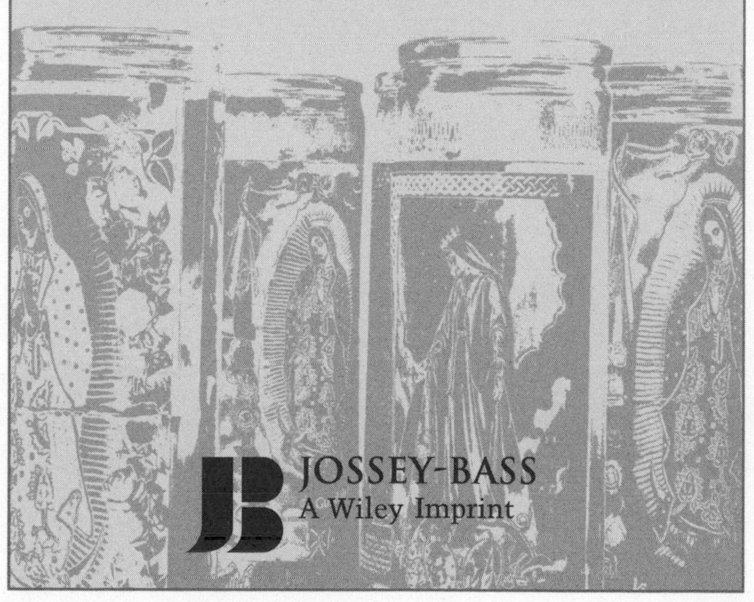

JOSSEY-BASS
A Wiley Imprint

Published by Jossey-Bass
A Wiley Imprint
989 Market Street, San Francisco, CA 94103-1741—www.josseybass.com

Interior image courtesy Joanne Clapp Fullagar

ISBN-13: 978-1-61523-304-5

Printed in the United States of America

CONTENTS

I dedicate this book to my mother and father,
who first taught me
to "dwell in the house of the LORD"
(Psalm 23:6)

INTRODUCTION

I did not step inside a Roman Catholic church until I was nineteen years old and living in a foreign country. A hyperreligious child and teenager, I grew up outside of Chicago in a town that was home to a lot of evangelical Protestants, a lot of Catholics, and few others. I was in the first group. We believed that Catholics were going to hell unless they found our brand of true salvation.

I was intrigued by Catholics when I was a boy. In vague terms, I understood that they were a part of something enormous, much larger and more ancient and mysterious than my own tradition, and that my own faith somehow derived from the Catholic one. I was taught that Catholics were the same as they had always been, going back centuries, and that they should have known better, long ago. Their spiritual practices intrigued me. I remember making fun of the kids on the playground who crossed themselves, mocking how they would do it in times of stress or anticipation, muttering short prayers, as I had seen it done by baseball players on television. "What is *that* all about?" I accused, rolling my eyes in as exaggerated a way as I could muster. It's a wonder that nobody ever punched me in the face. But I wasn't really malicious; I was like a child playing with something in order to understand it.

The rub is, of course, that I believed I was doing good. I was doing a perverse sort of "witnessing," or sharing of my faith—at least in the obnoxious manner of an adolescent. Later, while a student in Bible college in Chicago, I didn't do much better. My sarcastic teasing turned into manipulative cajoling, again because I thought I was doing good. While a freshman in Bible college, I trained to become a missionary to the Philippines, an overwhelmingly Catholic country. I was sent to be an assistant church planter (that's what we called it) and to help organize a youth group as part of the building of an evangelical Protestant congregation in the city of Batangas. The only people in Batangas available to convert to our brand of faith were Roman Catholics, and we tried.

It was while I was in the Philippines that I first walked into a Catholic church. My senses felt as if they might explode that afternoon. Sunlight poured in through tinted windows, and people were everywhere, in the pews, waiting for the confessional, lighting vigil candles in side chapels. No one made eye contact with me as they walked here and there; I stood in the middle of it all, staring at them.

I smelled incense wafting to the wooden rafters. I saw images and statues of saints, some of them with broken arms or ears missing. Many of them were carved in stone or molded in plaster, colored in ways that were largely unfamiliar to me, with tints of orange and yellow and blue that were paler but somehow livelier than what I had commonly seen in church. There were vessels of what I guessed held holy water, and I had no idea what that might mean, especially when the priests began tossing sprinkles of it on the heads of the congregation with what looked like brushes. And the people had the most intense looks on their faces. I had been taught that the pieties of Catholics, and the passion of their devotions, were part of the sadness of the Catholic story: they were misled into these spiritual beliefs and practices in place of knowing the real truth. All of that religion was supposed to somehow be bad. But what I saw that day began to change my heart and my mind.

I was, of course, a member of one of the "free" churches. We were able to do precisely and only what we wanted to do in our spirituality and worship. We were "free," right? Not so much. I realized while in Batangas that Christians around the world were celebrating something called Pentecost and that each week of Pentecost gradually circles us back around to Advent, when the church year begins all over again. The idea of celebrating the earthly events that make up our redemption—the Annunciation, the Nativity, the Flight into Egypt, the Crucifixion, the Day of Pentecost—was exciting to me.

I know plenty of people who are "spiritual and not religious" and many more who have discarded organized religion altogether because they have been hurt or have felt misled. I sympathize with all of them—I've been there myself. Spirituality is as full of promise as we ourselves are, and that usually feels good. Religion, meanwhile, will probably always be a mess, a lure for the power hungry, and hierarchical beyond all that seems reasonable. Nevertheless, I am spiritual and I also love religion. I love what Thomas Howard calls "the ancient Church and all that she holds for us in her liturgy, her teaching, her disciplines, her devotions, and her spiritual writings."[1] I love the sensuous, mysterious approach to faith that lands in the heart and the body as well as in the head.

I visited my first Catholic church because Catholic friends had invited me. I was there in Batangas to "save" them, but in the end, I felt that they saved me.

SECTION ONE

THE LANGUAGE AND THE SPIRIT

Forget What You Thought You Knew

> What people don't realize is how much religion costs. They think faith is a big electric blanket, when of course it is the cross. It is much harder to believe than not to believe.
>
> —Flannery O'Connor, Letter to Louise Abbot[1]

I don't want to convince you to become a Roman Catholic—I am in fact not one myself—but I *do* want you to join me in drinking deeply in the Catholic tradition. Why? Because Catholic spirituality is where so many of the riches lie.

With an Irish surname like Sweeney, you'd think I was already—rather than almost—Catholic. But no. My paternal grandparents both came from Catholic families, my grandfather's Irish and my grandmother's Italian. They all settled in Kansas and became farmers. It wasn't easy to be Catholic in Kansas in the 1800s, and so they turned Protestant.

Several years ago, I visited the small village in the Po River valley of Italy that my great-grandmother's family left in the 1890s in order to immigrate to America. We went to the Catholic church there to examine the baptismal records, only to learn that a fire a century ago had destroyed them. I wish I could click on YouTube and see a clip of my great-grandmother's baptism and First Communion in that old Italian church. Much of the original nave was destroyed in World War II, but the outer wall of rough stone rock remains. Such a foundation now cradles a newer timbered roof and freshly painted, movable pews where schoolgirls play with their rosaries and elderly women and men wait patiently for their turn at confession. The Catholic history of my ancestors haunts me, I suppose.

The most important reason for being a Christian must be to dedicate yourself to bringing about the kingdom of God: it's not primarily about what we believe or think or feel but more about what we actually do with our brains and hearts and bodies. But our focus in churches is rarely on these more practical, embodied ends of faith. In our denominations—which seem to multiply faster than rabbits—we like to defend our authority and sometimes our autonomy and prefer our worship, sacraments, and ways of doing things to those of others. The more time we spend trying to protect these fiefdoms of institution, the less time we spend doing the things that matter most, like feeding the hungry, caring for the needy, praying for our enemies, visiting those in prison, and showing love in myriad ways. We need to move beyond trying to save individual churches or traditions. We need to *be* church, instead, wherever we are and whomever we're with. And for that reason, I'm not very interested in buttressing any denomination. But I love the stuff and practices of what happens in religion—those millions of ways that actual churches instruct and guide us in the ways of God.

I've never been a big fan of religious authority, especially not when it is made out to be the stuff of foundational or even propositional truth—as if following Christ is impossible without first believing or doing this or that or the other thing. My love for religion does not mean that I love the hierarchical authority of faith. The cause of religion is always better served when authority is more leveled than hierarchical. Nevertheless, I respect the pope, both the position and the man. In his new book about Jesus of Nazareth, Benedict XVI writes, "It goes without saying that this book is in no way an exercise of the magisterium, but is solely an expression of my personal search. . . . Everyone is free, then, to contradict me. I would only ask my readers for that initial goodwill without which there can be no understanding."[2] Any non-Catholic who thinks that this pope is heavy-handed with authority simply is not paying attention.

Religion can still fool us into thinking that there are magic formulas for solving our problems. Standing in the way of spirituality are the many ways that we often remain beholden to the magic and taboos, pride and false gods that Jesus came to free us from. Catholics and Protestants alike down through the centuries—including people like Francis of Assisi, Erasmus and Martin Luther, Oscar Romero and Simone Weil, and Martin Luther King Jr.—have worked to keep these things out of faith. We are always set on by the money changers in the temple. Our Pharisees—the doctrine police—are always wanting to argue. Sacrifices offered to God, trying to appease God, sacrificing everything but the heart and will that God really wants. *We* are the problem, the reason why God's kingdom has not come, rather than others whom we might consider our more "secular" opponents. It is for these reasons that some Catholics will argue today that the trouble for religion, particularly in America, isn't that society is secular but perhaps that it isn't secular enough—and I think they are probably right. Our outward piety—demonstrated in church attendance and the talk in our public square—is first among nations, but why then are we also the world's most violent?

I remember the first time I visited Saint Peter's Basilica in Rome. I toured that incredible church and saw the huge tombs of popes and saints, reminiscent of the memorial grandeur that one sees in London's Westminster Abbey in honor of kings and queens. In Saint Peter's, I prayed at Michelangelo's *Pietà*. I sat at the back of a consecration Mass for new Italian priests. But then I went downstairs to the Vatican museums. Experts don't even know all that those corridors contain. The rare manuscripts on display are encrusted with jewels. Others are tucked in ancient closets far from the light of day. Saints' relics of bone and blood and things that were once touched are encased in gold. The treasure that is not on display there could fill the halls of the Louvre.

Like many people, I was simultaneously enthralled and disgusted by the wealth and power of the Vatican museums. But money and power are not what it means to be Catholic. If all of that wealth disappeared tomorrow, the storehouse of all things Catholic would still be one of the richest places on earth. The riches all originate in—and supply—our shared practice, history, and mystery.

In some of the explorations that follow, I will be reevaluating Catholicism. There have been many figures in history, including the first men and women who took to calling themselves Protestants, who became so caught up in battling the amassed wealth and power of the Catholic Church that they failed to remember and see what was more important beneath. There is so much beauty to be uncovered there, and there are many elements of Catholicism that (even unbidden) have potency for non-Catholics and for people who are not "Catholics in good standing," as the Roman Catholic Church would define it. You need to be willing—whether you were born into the Church and would call yourself "lapsed" or whether you have always been suspicious—to open your mind and heart.

Being Christian is not the same thing as being churchy or even religious. There are different layers to it, and some speak for our intentions, while others merely declare who we are, whether we intend it or not. The outer layer is to affirm the beliefs of the ancient church and to honor, love, and remember Christ in practice, liturgy, and worship. Many of us do that intentionally and visibly on a regular basis. My first encounter with Catholic worship was a profound one. For others, the outer layer may not mean very much.

But there is much more below that surface. The next layer down is where we encounter Christ. This is not about creeds. Creeds are ultimately unsatisfying to both believers and detractors because we do not encounter the Holy One in a creed. The way we believe or don't believe in the propositions of religion is entirely different from *faith*. When Hebrews says that faith is "evidence of things not seen," it doesn't say that faith is *believing in* evidence of things not seen. Faith is itself the evidence. Belief and assent are something else, but faith is borne in us. There are distinctively Catholic ways of faith and belief, which we'll discuss in detail in what follows.

To be Christian is to share in the mystery of being known by the person of Jesus who is loving us. And we do this in various ways and places—whether we know it or not. The problem is that many of us have been conditioned to discount, discredit, and deny this mystery in us. Catholic spirituality is all about responding to these mysteries—even though religious leaders have often said that being Catholic is primarily about that outer crust of religious observance, confusing the matter further.

Go another layer in, right to the center, and to be Christian is to be human. The message of the Incarnation is that the human being is a new species combining the earthly and the godly. There are biologists today who pinpoint the ways that spirituality has become part of the "natural state" of being human. The geneticist Dean Hamer has even identified God "genes" that he claims to have discovered using behavioral genetics and neurobiology to show that human brains inherit predispositions to embracing a higher power.[3] Spiritual or religious experience is said to be universally human and biologically natural. In other words, being Christian is being human.

Graham Greene suggested something similar in his novel *A Burnt-Out Case* decades ago. Here is part of a conversation between an atheist and a believer:

> "Evolution today can produce Hitlers as well as St. John of the Cross. I have a small hope, that's all, a very small hope, that someone they call Christ was the fertile element, looking for a crack in the wall to plant its seed.... Love is planted in many now, even uselessly in some cases, like an appendix. Sometimes of course people call it hate."
>
> "I haven't found any trace of it in myself."
>
> "Perhaps you are looking for something too big and too important. Or too active."[4]

Even Richard Dawkins, the famous religion hater, argues in *The God Delusion* that the stubborn persistence of belief in God down through the ages might have something to do with natural selection.[5] Who knows for sure, but we are unavoidably human, and on the deepest level, to be human is to be Christ—at least in some mute, inglorious ways. As the novelist Marilynne Robinson recently wrote, "I believe in the holiness of the human person and of humanity as a phenomenon."[6] Sometimes there is little visible or real difference between those of us who live consciously and deliberately in this and those of us who don't.

Even though being human and Christian is this inclusive, the language of being Catholic can still sometimes seem exclusive. There may not be a special handshake or code to be deciphered, but nevertheless, it takes time for the non-Catholic to feel comfortable in Catholic language, symbolism, and imagination.

The Israelites used a code word more than three thousand years ago to identify Ephraimite spies who were attempting to infiltrate Gilead after a battle. According to the book of Judges, this story is where the English word *shibboleth* originated. To identify the spies, the soldiers of Gilead asked each Ephraimite, as he tried to cross the Jordan River, to pronounce a word that the two tribes pronounced differently: "Gilead then cut Ephraim off from the fords of the Jordan, and whenever Ephraimite fugitives said, 'Let me cross,' the men of Gilead would ask, 'Are you an Ephraimite?' If he said, 'No,' they then said, 'Very well, say Shibboleth.' If anyone said, 'Sibboleth,' because he could not pronounce it, then they would seize him and kill him by the fords of the Jordan" (Judges 12:5–6). *Shibboleth* is the Hebrew word for a rushing stream.

Apart from the deadly intent, this might be akin today to someone in a bar across from Yankee Stadium trying to identify a clandestine Red Sox fan by asking him to speak. In speech, both fans would most likely "pahk their kahs" rather than "park their cars," but to the trained ear, there are subtle differences of pronunciation. The Dutch resistance used a shibboleth during World War II to find Nazi spies in their country; they found subtle ways to get men whom they suspected of spying to talk about Scheveningen, a seaside resort in the Netherlands frequented in those days by German tourists (the Germans and the Dutch pronounce the consonant cluster *sch* very differently).

In one of her short stories, Mary Gordon tells of a man who talks in a way that gives him away as a Catholic convert: "But the way Dr. Meyers said 'The Faith' made Joseph feel sorry for him. It was a clue, if anyone was looking for clues, that he had not been born a Catholic, and all those things that one breathed in at Catholic birth he'd had to learn, as if he had been learning a new language."[7] These chapters are my explorations of both the language and spirit of being Catholic.

"Catholic"

> "The Church is not a thing like the Athenaeum Club," he cried. "If the Athenaeum Club lost all its members, the Athenaeum Club would dissolve and cease to exist. But when we belong to the Church we belong to something which is outside all of us; which is outside everything you talk about, outside the Cardinals and the Pope. They belong to it, but it does not belong to them. If we all fell dead suddenly, the Church would still somehow exist in God."
>
> —G. K. CHESTERTON, *THE BALL AND THE CROSS*[8]

The word *catholic,* meaning "general" or "universal," was first applied to the early church in about A.D. 110 to distinguish the Christian faith from the Judaism out of which it sprang. First-century Judaism was centered on a specific people (the Israelites or Hebrews) and specific places (the Temple, the city of Jerusalem, the Promised Land, and other biblical sites). To define this new faith as "catholic" was to say that what Christ began was something different: it was available everywhere, easily transported, mostly invisible, universally understood, and not limited to one or a few nations, cultures, or languages. Somewhere along the way, over the course of the centuries, this broad understanding of being "catholic" transformed into a web of practices, creeds, and differentiated ways of believing embodied in the Roman Catholic (that is, Universal) Church.

Conversely, consider what it means to be Protestant. To be Protestant is to define yourself as protesting against certain forms of religion. The word *Protestant* began as a political moniker in the sixteenth century to describe the protestations of certain German princes at the Second Diet of Speyer, in the Rhineland of Germany. Soon afterward, the word took on a broader meaning for believers who wished to differ from the orthodoxy of the Roman Catholic Church. Some parts of the world still reveal the political origins of this disunion; we still unfortunately talk about Orthodox Serbs, Catholic Croats, and Ulster Protestants.

To my mind, there is little need for Protestants anymore. What are we still protesting? The Reformation of the sixteenth century was a European event. Just as Roman Catholicism was inevitably formed by Mediterranean sensibilities and ideas in the first few centuries after Jesus lived and died, the first waves of Reformation were formed by Germanic responses to late medieval corruption both in the Church and outside of it. Perhaps the cat is out of the bag and we'll never be able to catch it again.

The original, one, true Catholic Church is what compels many of us today, not protest. But what is that "one" and "true" Church? No one can say for sure, even though we try. As the fourth-century Nicene Creed affirms, "We believe in the one Holy Catholic and Apostolic Church." Anglicans,

Roman Catholics, and Orthodox all link their religious authority to the first twelve apostles of Christ. To be an "apostolic" church is to trace your authority to a long succession of ordained bishops all the way back to Bartholomew, Peter, John, or any of the other nine original apostles. But it's not that simple. In Catholic and some Orthodox parishes, those four words in the Creed—*Holy, Catholic, Apostolic, Church*—are capitalized, whereas in Anglican and Protestant churches, they are not. The new *Lutheran Service Book* even replaces the lowercased *catholic* with an uppercased *Christian*.

Ultimately, there is no longer such a thing as the "original" Church; we can't recover the ancient past, and if we did, we wouldn't necessarily want to replicate it anyway. When I say that the one, true Catholic Church is what compels many of us today, what I mean is that we desire more and more to be involved in something universal, vast, beyond us. We "evolved" Protestants desire to protest less by turning back to what is tried and true, part of the bigger story of what it means to be Christian. Thomas Howard explains this transition well when he says, "How much better it is to hand the immense task over to the venerable wisdom of the Church herself, so that the pattern of our interior life takes shape as a matter of obedience and not of our own devising."[9]

It is all things *Catholic* that bring us home to tradition, to the first centuries, to the faith in Christ that baffled and inspired Saint Paul; that seemed worth dying for in the Roman amphitheaters, built faith communities and churches all over the world, and formed the language of the Nicene Creed and the saints of the Middle Ages—the mysteries of faith that challenged the first millennium and challenge people today. Many Christians in the Global South—where both Catholicism and Protestantism have grown up indigenously and so resemble each other more than they do in Europe—seem to understand this better than we do.

I write this book with a religious identity that is thoroughly Christian, and yet indefinably so. My origins were evangelical Protestant and my early adulthood was a process of searching from one tradition to the next. But over the last two decades, I have gradually found my identity in the mystery of what is Catholic. I am drawn to the ancient and medieval traditions out of a desire to connect with the deepest and widest paths on the way. Two millennia of saints and practices and teachings and mystery form a golden string that connects us to our beginnings. These paths are very much about our future, even as they illuminate our past. If you are like me and seek a new set of practices and ways of thinking about your relationship with God—explore with me our ancient past and our necessary future.

I make the assumption that tradition and scripture are equally important. For centuries, Protestants have excitedly distinguished themselves from Catholics on the issues of justification by faith alone and *sola scriptura.* Martin Luther said, "Scripture is its own interpreter. . . . Scripture is itself its own light. It is therefore good when Scripture interprets itself."[10] But I agree with the poet Scott Cairns when he says, "It is good to note that even Martin Luther—the father of our cranky phrase, *sola scriptura*—was himself utterly well-equipped *with* and assisted *by* a rich and enriching communion with the tradition expressed by the fathers and mothers of the Church. Having thoroughly ingested that tradition, he was, perhaps, in a unique position to say he would thereafter proceed 'by scripture alone.' We and our interpretations, on the other hand, might fare better with a little company."[11] In other words, even the reformer needed to be Catholic in order to see things as clearly as he did.

And then there are those issues that Catholics get excited about in the reverse, such as the proper meaning of the sacraments and apostolic succession. In one direction or another, these issues have ushered good men and women into one denomination or another. But my reflections are for the purposes of stepping back from the old debates and looking at the beauty of ancient, shared faith. Like any good Catholic, I am occasionally protesting, but I am still Catholic in the broadest sense of the word. To be Christian is to be Catholic; whether you capitalize the *C* is a matter of where your heart is.

Almost Catholic begins in Section One with new definitions and language. Section Two is all about what I call "The Catholic Imagination," exploring a particular way of seeing the world. Section Three takes a look at the most important single aspect of what it means to be Catholic, which is to embrace the Incarnate Christ. The Incarnation is what links us essentially to Jesus, and I find many aspects of that earthiness to be more compelling than God's otherworldliness. Section Four enters into the small things I love that fill my Catholic life with physical connections to reality. Section Five offers a short and slightly unorthodox catechesis—a meaningful, living transmission of the faith—that reflects my own journey of understanding. Finally, Section Six offers several practices on the well-worn path that pull us together. Practices such as these are often called "ancient-future," symbolizing the ways in which they are being rediscovered by many people today. I find that exciting.

Forget About Conversion

> [He] had been visited in all his senses: touched as by an unction on his cruel eyes that had not seen the countenance of pardon; on his inattentive ears, which had not heard the groaning of the Holy Spirit; on his wild-beast nostrils, which had not perceived the fragrant odor of the divine rapture; on the sepulcher of his mouth, which had not eaten the living bread; on his violent hands, which had not helped to carry the Savior's cross; on his impatient feet, which had hastened in all directions, except towards the holy sepulcher. That word *conversion,* so often prostituted, if applied to him, did not altogether explain the catastrophic change.
>
> —Léon Bloy, *The Woman Who Was Poor*[12]

I have just turned forty. It's important to point that out, because you are reading a book of musings on beliefs and practices that are ancient in origin but still held dear by many people, perhaps even by you. Being forty (too young to understand much, too old to really know), I probably experience these things in ways that say something about my generation.

I believe that the practice, history, and mystery of Catholic faith are for everyone. You don't need a special password to come in. There is no secret code. And you don't have to be *Roman* to practice spirituality that is Catholic. To be Catholic is a conscious choice, but it is not the same thing as being born into Roman Catholicism or even converting to it.

Conversion was all the rage in my parents' generation. Dabbling with a tradition was frowned on, whereas taking the conversion plunge was respectable. Even movements from one denomination to another—which seem today like selecting a different mode of transportation on the way to worship—became conversions. Over the years, I've watched friends and family convert from Baptist to Presbyterian, from Dutch Reformed to Missouri Synod Lutheran to Evangelical Lutheran, and bigger jumps, such as from Methodist to Anglican to Eastern Orthodox or Roman Catholicism, and so on. Each movement involves more than simply changing seats or buildings. They include catechisms, orientation and confirmation classes, and elaborate ceremonies.

The convert is always the most earnest and determined of practitioners. Some converts to Roman Catholicism will say that theirs was a decision made after becoming convinced of truth. They were convinced that Roman Catholicism is the oldest tradition in Christendom. They read the arguments for the apostolic succession that traces itself back to Saint Peter. Such thinking convinced thousands of people during the last century toward Roman Catholicism, drawn by the desire to connect with absolute and immutable Truth and Tradition. Their beliefs took on institutional importance in their lives.

I don't seek Truth with a capital *T.* For one thing, I believe that faith usually happens in much more haphazard fashion. There will always be stories of Christians who consider the arguments on both sides, like Justice weighing her scales, and then favor Christianity as most true. But for every one of these today, there are three who enter by a side door. A friend helps in a time of crisis and shows you how to pray. A local parish opens its doors at a time when you need to get warm. Perhaps even something inexplicable happens to you—call it spiritual experience—and it begins to make sense to explore more of that sort of thing with like-minded others. Becoming a person of faith takes a lifetime, and it begins far more often in participation than it does in some sort of judging. The French philosopher Blaise Pascal criticized the approach to faith that says it begins with belief. You start with belonging, he said. Belief comes later, and even then, belief comes and goes. Consistent belief is not essential to faith.

Also, I think that Christians today are beginning to accept that *not* knowing is actually essential to faith. Our premodern ancestors understood this instinctually. That was when mystery permeated everything. They didn't presume much knowledge at all. But during the Middle Ages, that same power of mystery was used by the powerful against the weak. The poor were made poorer when their religious leaders created indulgences (pardons for sins) that could be purchased, Masses for the dead that were also bought, payments for the right to Baptism, First Communion, and Confirmation. Understanding those abuses are where most Protestants stop in coming to know Catholicism.

The abuses of the past led to the promises of reformation and enlightenment and ultimately to where we find ourselves today: feeling that we are the ultimate judges of what is true and what is not. It all reminds me of one of the stories from the enigmatic monks known as the Desert Fathers (because they fled the cities of ancient Egypt to lead a different sort of life in the desert). Saint Antony once posed a question to the gathering of followers that had grown up around him. He quoted them a difficult passage from the Bible, and then he asked each in turn, "What does this mean?" From the youngest to the eldest, the men offered erudite and subtle readings of the ancient text. Each of them believed that their answers would show their learning and earnestness for the spiritual life. But the last to respond was a monk named Joseph. When Antony asked him for the meaning of the verse, Joseph said very simply, "I do not know." At that, Antony told the gathered disciples, "Only Joseph knows the way."

To look at faith through the lens of belief is to be stuck in some sort of rationalism that makes little sense today. William Blake said that our reason—those "mind-forg'd manacles"—will undo us as Christians and as human beings.[13]

Whatever category of Christian you are, chances are good that you've been taught to be confident in the power of believing and in your ability to identify and discover truth as a buttress for belief. This is the way of modernity that we inherited from the Enlightenment. Modernity convinced our ancestors that religious faith should be replaced by reason so that a more reliable truth could take its place. But take a quick look at our recent past, and it is easy to lose confidence in those promises. What have three hundred years of modernity—from about 1650 to about 1950—accomplished for us? Plenty of good, but we have also seen that modernity is no savior. Science promised to save humanity and has created ever-greater ways to destroy us. Economic systems such as capitalism and Marxism offered security for all, but instead the gap widens between the ridiculously rich and the horribly poor year by year. Politics claimed that it would find ways to provide for people; instead, it most often breeds greed and feeds on power.

Modernity is based on the ideas that faith will always succumb to reason, but of course, it doesn't. As Henry Adams said long ago, it is faith that holds up the buttresses of the Gothic churches: without faith they'd make no sense, but within faith, the universe that includes them is marvelous, mysterious, and tapped into something that secularism can't fathom.[14]

Many of us today acknowledge that we live in a new era—some call it *postmodernity*—in which propositional truth, certainty, and even papal infallibility play the same sort of smaller role in a spiritual life that they played in the pre-modern worldview. We decide what is true in different ways. The Christian writer and activist Brian McLaren recently wrote, "How do you know if something is true? First, you engage in spiritual *practices* like prayer, Bible reading, forgiveness, and service. Then you see what happens; you remain open to *experience.* Finally, you report your experience to others in the field of spirituality for their *discernment,* to see if they confirm your findings or not."[15]

We have immersed ourselves in the protests and reason of reformations and enlightenment. It is time to move on. The meaning of life—as well as faith—has little to do with truth and answering the "big" questions and has a lot to do with actually doing away with the questions. Life and faith are about living in ways that make believing easier and make doing for others normal.

For me, qualities such as hoping, desiring, and reconciling have taken on bigger roles in my life as the energy

I used to pour into believing has moved more and more into the background. Hope is not optimism. Love is not affection. To feel or show optimism and affection is pretty simple, but to hope and love takes time, practice, and self-examination. Capacities such as hope are to be learned and strengthened—and I find them recommended in the scriptures more often than belief. Even when Jesus praises belief, as in the case of the woman who anointed his feet with tears and alabaster (and "who had a bad name in town"), he praises her desire and love, not the sort of propositional belief that we have come to understand today. "I tell you that her sins, many as they are, have been forgiven her, because she has shown such great love" (Luke 7:36–47).

When Edith Stein first read the autobiography of Saint Teresa of Avila, she stayed up all night, engrossed. It was through Teresa that Stein first met a God who was real. Afterward, she felt the divine presence so clearly that she said she felt absolutely compelled to become a Christian, even a Roman Catholic, and eventually a Carmelite nun. *That* is the sort of conversion I can understand. I've never had that complete an experience. In the meantime, for many of the rest of us, paradoxes often remain the best answers.

I sometimes wonder if the animal or insect or invertebrate worlds are as perplexed these days as we humans find ourselves. I suppose not, but we have the burden of reflection forced on us. Conversion is sometimes used as a way of ending an argument. It's a conclusion—staking one's flag in the ground, and it feels good. But my spiritual life is not ready for any conclusions, at least not yet.

Doubters and Believers, Atheists and Agnostics

"I rather believe in doubting. The only people I've met in this world who never doubt are materialists and atheists."

—MALCOLM MUGGERIDGE, "HOW DOES ONE FIND FAITH?"[16]

"We want a few mad people now. See where the sane ones have landed us!"

—GEORGE BERNARD SHAW, *SAINT JOAN*[17]

Catholic spirituality and practice not only allow doubt, misbelief, and the refusal to believe but in many ways encourage them! In fact, the so-called lapsed Catholic is often the most concerned of all people when it comes to matters of faith. Why else would they call themselves "lapsed" if they were not conscious of the ideal? One of the surest signs of an inner spiritual life is the frustration, anger, and enthusiasm of the lapsed, the doubter, the one who has intentionally put himself or herself on the outside looking in.

Doubt is the most powerful fuel to faith. Even when doubt batters belief (our ability to agree that something is true) like a ship at sea during a nor'easter—even then, doubt fuels faith, our wanting to believe. I feel far more comfortable with people who have doubted than I do with those for whom belief always seems to be a lock. Any person who troubles with matters of religion enough to fight against them is someone in whom the spirit is hard at work. I would rather have the pews full of angry atheists and questioning agnostics than of certain or sleepy believers on any given Sunday or Saturday night.

Doubting Thomas—the one disciple who insisted on sticking his finger into the wounds of Christ—should inspire us to similarly test and challenge what we are told. We are people with skin and beating hearts, not disembodied spirits, and we want to know what's what as sure as we possibly can.

Why is it that we don't hear Methodists and Quakers and Congregationalists describe themselves as "lapsed"? The average Protestant will use the term *inactive* rather than *lapsed*, or perhaps even *former.* But to be Catholic is to be a part of something self-defining, something enormous, far bigger than precepts of belonging to a local church could ever communicate. It's only the feeling of obligation that has left the lapsed. They are still looking. The novelist Graham Greene took to calling himself a "Catholic agnostic" and even a "Catholic atheist" toward the end of his life.[18] Greene was communicating the deep divide that he felt between faith and belief. He had plenty of the first and less and less of the second.

The British broadcaster John Humphrys hosted a popular BBC TV show a few years ago called *In Search of God.* Humphrys, who describes himself as a former Roman Catholic, approaches matters of faith with profound skepticism, energy, and creativity. He interviewed the archbishop of

Canterbury, the chief rabbi of Great Britain, and the atheist former Muslim scholar Tariq Ramadan, posing challenging questions to each of these men, and the result was interesting television. A year later, Humphrys followed up the television series with a book titled *In God We Doubt: Confessions of an Angry Agnostic.*[19] In doubting reflections such as his, you may find more meaningful spirituality and faith than in many of the pious books that glow on the shelves of religious bookshops.

"Mortal eyes cannot distinguish the saint from the heretic," says one accuser of Joan of Arc in George Bernard Shaw's *Saint Joan*.[20] Indeed, when it comes to faith, it can be nearly impossible to tell the difference between the two. It's not as if you can spot a follower of Christ the same way you spot a deer in the woods. We don't wear badges or even head scarves, although we are supposed to be doing certain things that make it easier to find us.

If you asked a hundred people what it means to be Christian, they'd give you a hundred different answers. But most would likely say, "I go to church" or "I go to such-and-such church." "My parents were Christian." And "I was raised a Christian. I was baptized when I was young." Does any of that ultimately matter? The follower of Christ is not necessarily a person that you would expect to meet in church.

Consider the example of Mohandas Gandhi. Many Christian observers in India eighty years ago thought that they saw Saint Francis of Assisi in Mohandas Gandhi. Gandhi never renounced his Hinduism, but he often declared himself a follower of Jesus Christ. He studied the Gospels and lived by them, carefully. There were times during the 1920s and 1930s when Gandhi would arrive to give a lecture and would simply quote from the New Testament, usually from the Sermon on the Mount and the Beatitudes. On one occasion he did this and said, "That is my address to you. Act upon that." A Hindu intellectual of the 1920s said about Gandhi: "What the [Christian] missionaries have not been able to do in fifty years Gandhi by his life and trial and incarceration has done, namely, he has turned the eyes of India toward the cross."[21] It is ironic but true that Gandhi may have been a more faithful follower of Christ than many Christians have been.

Millions of the lapsed and doubting are now creating new-old ways to be Christian and Catholic or just to be believers. As many as five million are involved in house churches in the United States alone, and these are mostly evangelical Christians. Other lay movements such as the Community of Sant'Egidio (Catholic, founded by high school students in 1968 and now numbering more than fifty thousand adherents in seventy countries) and the Focolare Movement (of Catholic origin but broadly ecumenical today; founded in 1943, now with more than five million members) draw people who often feel uncomfortable in traditional churches, even as they want the practice, history, and mystery of faith.

Even great saints of history were sometimes "lapsed," going through their own rebellions, rejections, reformations—whatever you want to call them—before arriving at other ways of doing religion. Francis and Clare of Assisi, for instance, each rejected their mothers and fathers as they went in search of a more meaningful relationship with their heavenly father. Francis literally disowned his father in one of the piazzas of Assisi, and Clare fled home in the middle of the night. What would we think of these rebellions today? Sometimes we see ourselves and others as lapsed or doubting simply because we don't have the benefit of hindsight.

Eleven Steps to Becoming a Truly Catholic Christian

"I'll become a Catholic. What does one have to do?"

. . . "Very well," she said, "I will see about having you instructed."

"Look, . . . I haven't the time. Instruction will be wasted on me. Just you give me the form and I'll sign on the dotted line."

"It usually takes some months—often a lifetime."

—EVELYN WAUGH, *BRIDESHEAD REVISITED*[22]

With more than a nod to the phrasings of the original twelve steps used in Alcoholics Anonymous, I call these "Eleven Steps to Becoming a Truly Catholic Christian." If you can join in most of these shared statements, you are well on your way!

1. We acknowledge that our faith is larger than ourselves.
2. We believe that unity with two millennia of believers and spiritual practices is more important than faith by ourselves.
3. Our catholicity leads us to embrace those who differ from us, which is difficult, because the same catholicity leads us to seek unity more often than reform.
4. We seek to work for the kingdom of God here and now, uncovering what is sacred in the world around us, working to lift and redeem all things.
5. We seek to see the world as it is, to see the truth as clearly as we are able, with the help of the Holy Spirit. We regularly admit to God, to ourselves, and to other human beings the nature of our sins and weaknesses.
6. We regularly pray for forgiveness for our trespasses against God and others, and we also pray regularly for those who trespass against us.
7. We practice faith that unites heaven and earth, time and eternity: seeking the company of saints, remembering Christ's death and Resurrection in the liturgy, reading the scriptures, with prayers old and new, and supporting others.
8. We support each other in both faith and doubt, understanding that both are essential to spiritual maturity.
9. We regularly try to believe the unbelievable and to talk openly, but never combatively, about these things with others.
10. We look for ways to open ourselves and experience at first hand the infinite ways that Christ lives in and through people who are different from ourselves. Saint Paul said, "Do not quench the Spirit. Do not despise prophetic utterances. Test everything; retain what is good. Refrain from every kind of evil" (1 Thessalonians 5:19–22).
11. We order our days with spiritual practices that unite us with Catholics around the world.

SECTION TWO

THE CATHOLIC IMAGINATION

God Is Here

JOAN: I hear voices telling me what to do. They come from God.

ROBERT: They come from your imagination.

JOAN: Of course. That is how the messages of God come to us.

—GEORGE BERNARD SHAW, *SAINT JOAN*[1]

I used to live my life entirely from within what I would call a Protestant worldview that sees humanity as essentially separated from God. Protestants tend to emphasize the gulf that divides us, emphasizing how right belief may bridge the gap. It was once just me and my Bible and my pastor, discerning the truth—or so I thought at the time. But in fact, I simply had not yet discovered the teachers and saints who already surrounded me, the tradition that supported me, and the myriad ways that God was not separated from me but woven into all of my relationships.

Today, I try to live more in what I imprecisely call the "Catholic imagination." The Catholic imagination sees humanity as united with God in Christ through the

Incarnation. A Catholic mind looks for what binds us together more often than it attempts to examine what differentiates us from each other. It sees the world as a place where God is actively reconciling human beings and all of creation to himself. The Catholic imagination expects that all people will join in the essential work of reconciling, which extends to all marginalized people. In our own age, this means illegal immigrants, the homeless, prisoners, asylum seekers, gay and lesbian people, and the unborn. The Catholic way is to see what is happening, often beneath the surface, and to work for what is possible in the kingdom of God here on earth.

A Catholic worldview is one where physical appearances do not exactly explain themselves. Catholics naturally accept mysteries—in fact, they are plentiful. What we are, what any things are, is ultimately unknown to us. There is an essence to each thing that it strives to become in purer and purer forms. Flannery O'Connor once explained that as a Catholic novelist, she works at "seeing near things with their extensions of meaning and thus of seeing far things close up."[2]

In the Catholic imagination, what may otherwise appear to be cold, consumerist, or empty becomes a divine-human, heavenly-earthly experience. For example, theologians once argued about how many angels could stand on the point of a needle precisely because they lived in a universe where angels could inhabit special places! To be Catholic is to see things that others miss. There are some people, including some religious people, who live as if earthly existence is everything. Their imaginations are like their lives: temporal. The Spanish philosopher Miguel de Unamuno once said of these people, "Do they *really* exist? I think not. For if they existed, if they really existed, they would suffer from existing and they would not be content with it. If they truly existed in time and space, they would suffer from not existing in eternity and infinity."[3]

The modern mind finds it hard to imagine deity in these places of everyday life. "Show it to me," we demand. We can end up living almost literally in different worlds based on how we answer the most basic of questions, "Where do you live?"

Many obstacles have derailed what was once the premodern, more Catholic belief that God is among us. The Divine was believed to drop in from time to time to do inexplicable things, often at the request of the penitent. Spatial geography was different in those days too. Our ancestors looked exclusively up to the heavens to pray.

Before Christ, both sun and full moon were happy pronouncements of Divine intent. People looked at the heavens and earth knowing that God was responsible for those things that he angrily told Job out of the whirlwind:

> Where were you when I laid the foundation of the earth? Tell me, if you have understanding. . . . Who stretched the line upon it? On what were its bases sunk, or who laid its cornerstone when the morning stars sang together and all the heavenly beings shouted for joy? Or who shut in the sea with doors when it burst out from the womb? [Job 38:4–8].[4]

Enigmatic Irish saints set off in leather boats looking for the Deity in the deep, intrigued by more of God's words to Job: "Have you entered into the springs of the sea, or walked in the recesses of the deep?" (Job 38:16).

The medieval *Voyage of Saint Brendan* notes that "from time to time the wind filled their sails though they knew not whence it came or whither it was taking them."[5]

At the touch of God's finger, storms arose: "Can you lift up your voice to the clouds, so that a flood of waters may cover you?" (Job 38:34).

The divine maker even once knew what was in our very minds: "Who has put wisdom in the inward parts, or given understanding to the mind?" (Job 38:36).

This world of premodern, magical realism is long gone. And thank God for that; it was never very Christian anyway. The magical realist world began to depart at about the same time that the world began to reject the Copernican view of the universe. If the earth is no longer the center of the universe, then how can human beings be the center of a cosmic drama?

Behind the scenes all along was the most ancient root of the meaning of life from the first chapter of the Torah, when "God created man in the image of himself" (Genesis 1:27). The *imago dei,* or "image of God," described in Genesis is like a mirror that we may look into and see God reflected in our moral, spiritual, or intellectual activity. Adam being created in the *imago dei* had nothing to do with a man being God incarnate, however. That would come later. The New Testament compares God to a shepherd caring for his sheep, a hen gathering her brood, a father welcoming back his repentant son. These are all intimate images, but none as intimate as what would come.

"Behold a virgin shall conceive, and bear a son, and his name shall be called Emmanuel" (Matthew 1:23; compare Isaiah 7:14). The Jewish name Emmanuel means "God with us." Tradition says that Mary was reading the prophecy of Isaiah at the moment that Gabriel swooped down into her life. Emmanuel, "God with us." This was the name given to Jesus, and it promised salvation but also the presence of God in Christ.

The world that you were born into, that you awoke into this morning, is made sacred by the presence of God in Christ. The premodern worldview that believed easily in

God's presence everywhere and in everything was renewed and deepened at the Nativity. We are only beginning to understand what the presence of God in humanity is all about, but it is surely different from the more superstitious presence imagined by the writer of the book of Job.

When I answer the question of where I live, I see a universe somehow created and sustained by divine activity. I'm in a holy place where God is, and so are the saints of old, along with mud, flowers, snakes, angels and spiders, cancer and healings from cancer, all in one inexplicable mess. I am trying to understand these mysteries, but that's where I live. I live with pain because I am human. I love as a human who also knows divine love. I love where I am on this earth, but I know there is more than what is earthly and I am a part of that too. And for that knowledge, I am sometimes in pain and longing.

Sacred Spaces and Places

> "It is a curious thing . . . how your mind is supersaturated with the religion in which you say you disbelieve."
>
> —JAMES JOYCE, *A PORTRAIT OF THE ARTIST AS A YOUNG MAN*[6]

The Catholic imagination is not the same thing as the imaginations of individual Catholics. For many people at weekly Mass, the world looks about the same as it does to the woman eating a muffin and drinking a latte at Starbucks on Sunday morning. But for others, it is different. And it isn't necessary to be baptized Roman Catholic in order to see the world through Catholic eyes and live in ways that are Catholic.

Pierre Teilhard de Chardin, a French Jesuit priest and scientist in the twentieth century, became discouraged by the narrow forms and idioms of his Roman Catholicism and declared, "I am hyper-Catholic."[7] He wanted his faith to be a part of something broader, as it once was in the ancient and medieval church. He wasn't advocating for a circling of the wagons; instead, he meant big and boundary-breaking.

This sort of desire is why I love the Gothic revival architecture that began more than a century ago. An imprecise yearning for the synthesis and simplicity of the Middle Ages overtook literature (the *Waverley* novels of Sir Walter Scott), art criticism (John Ruskin), and spirituality as many Protestants in Europe and America were drawn to Catholicism. "Catholic" does not equal "medieval" by any stretch of the imagination; but Gothic architecture does seem to communicate the Catholic imagination in a profound way. The sociologist Robert Scott recently wrote:

> Because a main aim of the Gothic style was to flood the interior with light, builders had to devise new ways of constructing vaults, buttresses, and arches that would allow them to open the side walls for windows. . . . In medieval theology God concealed Himself so as to be revealed, and light was the principal and best means by which humans could know Him. . . . As the worshipers' eyes rose toward heaven, God's grace, in the form of sunlight, was imagined to stream down in benediction, encouraging exaltation. Sinners could be led to repent and strive for perfection by envisioning the world of spiritual perfection where God resided—a world suggested by the geometric regularity of cathedrals.[8]

To be Catholic is to live in the largest of all possible worlds. This includes spanning time (as in loving saints, remembering previous teachings, and observing revered traditions and sacraments), reorienting space (an ecumenical approach to all people, nations, and species), and changing within (always beginning in your own place and "neighborhood"). The Catholic imagination reaches back to the catacombs when Christians first began to seek faith mediated through symbol, art, sacrament, scripture, and the mystical oneness of community—rather than the secular one, focused on individual priorities, those of my clan, and perhaps a god or gods.

Ancient Celtic myths tell of thin places in the universe where the Divine is most present or closest. The veil of what separates us from the Divine is most easily penetrated in these locations, they say. You may have had similar feelings in certain places.

It may be true. I've felt it too. But Jesus reminded the world that God is found in human beings. Sacred spaces are not in the clouds or open fields so much as in humankind and the places where we gather together. *We* are where God is: in the interactions between us; inside of us; in the very incarnate stuff that we and our troubles are made of. We cannot always see clearly in that *imago dei* mirror, however. You won't know it simply by looking around. Instead, to be Catholic is, first, to be illuminated by the Holy Spirit. Ask and it shall be given to you. Ask and you shall know God with you, God with others, God made flesh in humankind. Ask and you will see it.

The Catholic brings to every problem and situation the perspective of trying to understand the human condition in light of God with us in Christ. The Catholic imagination sees the world from a perspective that is messy and particular and mystical. God is here. God is with us. We are generalists.

Before Raïssa and Jacques Maritain converted to Catholicism, Raïssa explains in her memoirs, one of their handicaps in accepting the Catholic worldview was that "our reason was equipped to destroy, not to construct."[9] So was mine. A Protestant mind wants to pull strands apart, dissecting and critiquing them, while the Catholic mind winds strands together. Take their different approaches to understanding a portion of scripture, for instance. The Protestant approach might be to break down the verses into phrases, analyzing the original languages, and applying some modest textual criticism to show how what was once said may be applied to today's situations. The Catholic approach might be to move in the opposite direction—to move from the tiny to the vast—and to illuminate the passage's meaning through comparison with other texts, the lives of people who have lived those texts, and other resources of tradition.

The imaginer stands in the middle of all things, past, present, and future, God-soaked truth and confusion alike, as a participant in an ancient story. To know something is not a job for the brain by itself but also the heart and the body. In this way, most of the oldest religious icons have no frames. You are not looking at a neatly framed representation but standing before a figure who is actually present. You are both there together. You can reach out to the Virgin and ask for her prayers. You can pray with downcast eyes with Saint Julian of Norwich. You can listen to the birds, hushed, as Saint Francis of Assisi speaks.

The presence of Christ also illuminates the spaces that we move in. We use spiritual practices as reminders of these things. This is why I love and admire the Catholic worldview—for its ability to redeem what is ordinary and make it extraordinary. Holy water fills the fonts at the entrances of churches, reminding us of our baptism. We dip our fingers in, making the sign of the cross from the forehead to the chest and from shoulder to shoulder, acknowledging the sacredness of entering into God's presence:

Forehead (mind)
Chest (heart)
Shoulder, shoulder (soul, strength)

To genuflect upon entering church, before the Holy Eucharist, is another simple way of reminding ourselves of the presence we stand in. Genuflection is done by touching the right knee to the floor while making the sign of the cross. The same holy water may fill fonts in our homes as well. To bless oneself when leaving the house or before saying special prayers is to become the "domestic church," recognizing our role in building faith through the sacred ordinariness of life, the stability of family and relationships, and work in our communities to help those who pattern the life of Christ in their very weaknesses.

All of this is perhaps best summarized in the words of one of the medieval mystics, Meister Eckhart. Eckhart was a German Dominican who taught that the real meaning of Christmas is not only that God's Son was born in a stable but that Christ is born in us. His most famous sermon, usually presented first in collections of his writings, was preached on Christmas morning. He begins with this summary:

> Here in time we celebrate the eternal birth that God the Father bore and still bears constantly in eternity, and which is also now born in time, in human nature. Saint Augustine says that this birth is happening continually. We should ask ourselves: If it doesn't happen in me, what good is that birth after all? What ultimately matters is that God's birth should happen in me.[10]

What I really love about the Catholic mystics, ancient, medieval, and modern, is how they can think abstractly and physically at the same time. Eckhart meant what he said on that Christmas morning quite literally and physically—that just as a baby was born in a stable long ago, a small fragment or spark or seed of God in Christ is born in each human being. That holy, inexplicable but physical reality may grow or not grow, depending in part on us. He is often waiting for us. Saint John of the Cross added to these descriptions by saying that in order to apply the meaning of Christmas, we must allow Mary and Joseph to stop from their wandering in Bethlehem and permit Christ to be born in our humble stable. These are the sorts of exercises that the Catholic imagination fills you with. They take time to make sense in a life. To understand the sacredness of our lives, our very bodies, and the places filled by God takes time.

Privy to a Revealed Secret

"I suppose they try and make you believe an awful lot of nonsense?"

"Is it nonsense? I wish it were. It sometimes sounds terribly sensible to me."

"But, my dear Sebastian, you can't seriously *believe* it all."

"Can't I?"

"I mean about Christmas and the star and the three kings and the ox and the ass."

"Oh yes, I believe that. It's a lovely idea."

"But you can't believe things because they're a lovely idea."

"But I do. That's how I believe."

—Evelyn Waugh, *Brideshead Revisited*[11]

In Oscar Hijuelos's novel *Mr. Ives' Christmas,* we follow the up-and-down life of the devout Catholic Edward Ives. Ives loves the Christmas season, reveling in its rituals and joy each year until his seventeen-year-old son is murdered just before the holiday in a random and senseless act of street violence in New York City in 1967. Just before that event, Ives has a vision—an everyday, ordinary look around—into the real world in which he exists but has never quite realized before.

At the corner of Madison Avenue and Forty-First Street in Manhattan, Ives "blinked his eyes and, in a moment of pure clarity that he would always remember, began to feel *euphoric,* all the world's goodness, as it were, spinning around him." The moment of epiphany continues for several minutes. "And in those moments he could feel the very life in the concrete below him, the ground humming—pipes and tangles of cables and wires beneath him, endless ticking, moving, animated objects. Why, it was as if he could hear molecules grinding, light shifting here and there, the vibrancy of things and spirit everywhere." Ives began to experience a love for all things and all people that he saw before him on the street that afternoon, in the bustling before-Christmas busyness near Macy's. "In the glow of such feelings people truly seemed blessed; truck and car horns sounded like heavenly trumpets, the murmur of the crowds and all the other voices fell upon his ears like music. . . . To hear, to smell, to see, to feel, all were miraculous."[12]

Have you ever been blessed with a similar experience, even if just for a moment?

This sort of vision involves both seeing and willing ourselves to see the secret of life laid out before us. One of the popular chants in a Taize-style prayer service goes, "I am sure I shall see the goodness of the Lord in the land of the living." We wouldn't have to say "I am sure" at the start of that chant if we were not just a little bit unsure. It is a hope and a wish at the same time.

Thomas Merton had the same sort of experience on a city street in Louisville, Kentucky. More than sixteen years after joining the Trappist monks of Our Lady of Gethsemane and long after his best-selling memoir, *The Seven Storey*

Mountain, had made him the most famous monk of the twentieth century, Merton suddenly saw the world as it really was. In his memoir, Merton wrote enthusiastically about how monks are men who have rejected the world so as to embrace it more profoundly, in prayer. A monk is a man who turns away from the world of people and chaos and things in order to dedicate himself to praying for the salvation of that same world. That was his understanding for the first decade and a half in the monastery.

But on March 18, 1958—he recorded the day and its profound meaning for his life—Merton was in Louisville on a rare visit to the city. Walking down the street toward the busy corner of Fourth Avenue and Walnut, he suddenly realized that he loved all of the people before him.

> I was suddenly overwhelmed with the realization that I loved all these people, that they were mine and I theirs, that we could not be alien to one another even though we were total strangers. It was like waking from a dream of separateness, of spurious self-isolation in a special world, the world of renunciation and supposed holiness. The whole illusion of a separate holy existence is a dream. Not that I question the reality of my vocation, or of my monastic life: but the conception of "separation from the world" that we have in the monastery too easily presents itself as a complete illusion. . . . We are in the same world as everybody else, the world of the bomb, the world of race hatred, the world of technology, the world of mass media, big business, revolution, and all the rest. This sense of liberation from an illusory difference was such a relief and such a joy to me that I almost laughed out loud. To think that for sixteen or seventeen years I have been taking seriously this pure illusion that is implicit in so much of our monastic

> thinking. I have the immense joy of being man, a member of a race in which God Himself became incarnate. As if the sorrows and stupidities of the human condition could overwhelm me, now I realize what we all are. And if only everybody could realize this! But it cannot be explained. There is no way of telling people that they are all walking around shining like the sun.[13]

The nameless faces of men and women going to and from their responsibilities—he adored them with a love that was not his own but a gift from God. Even as a cloistered, contemplative monk—or perhaps especially because he was contemplative—Merton realized on that day and that street corner that he was not separated from anyone but united essentially with every other human being. His spiritual practice changed on that afternoon as he began to realize the essential oneness of all people. No longer was he looking out from his monastic cell onto a world that needed his prayers. After his epiphany moment, Merton sought to be in solidarity with people of all backgrounds; he worked to understand others and to speak, pray, and act in unity with them. His practice could no longer be solitary. It wouldn't make sense.

The revealed secret is uncomplicated. It is simply that we are essentially one, a communion of saints. With the help of the Holy Spirit, we can know it and perhaps even see it. This is an aspect of Catholic spirituality that makes many Protestants nervous because down deep, we are all supposed to be mystics or at least contemplatives. Bernard of Clairvaux says that there are three types of kisses: "Kisses to the feet are for reconciliation. Kisses to the hand are for reward. And kisses that are mouth to mouth, for contemplation. We perceive what is hidden only through this third kiss."[14] Too often the Protestant imagination has trouble accepting that, wanting faith to be more reasonable, more sober, and more critical.

William Blake believed that reason stands in the way of inspiration and that churches have used reason as a sort of tyranny over the people. He'd have a lot of people agreeing with him today. "The idiot Reasoner laughs at the Man of Imagination," he wrote.[15] Blake lived what might be called a charmed life. He worked hard as an engraver and a painter, selling his work to pay his rent and support his wife and children. But in many respects, he lived in the world of eternity, in a universe filled with divine activity. He lived where I would like to live too.

In one poetic book of verse and engravings called *The Marriage of Heaven and Hell,* he was able to imagine the voice of the devil, walking among the fires of hell, dining with the prophets Isaiah and Ezekiel. He talked with angels and saw saints around him. We would lock him up today! But I don't believe that Blake's imagination was so far-fetched. I think he was simply more attuned than most of the rest of us to what *is.* He saw his work in the world as related entirely to expanding the imaginations of others:

> To open the Eternal Worlds, to open the immortal Eyes
> Of Man inwards into the Worlds of Thought, into Eternity
> Ever expanding in the Bosom of God, the Human Imagination.[16]

Nocturnal animals see best at nighttime. Their eyes are larger than those of other animals, and their retinas are made up almost entirely of rods instead of cones; this means that they can see in scant patches of light but they are colorblind. But that's not all. Their eyes also have a thick membrane, absent from other animals, that sends whatever small light is available back to the retina for a second time. In other words, nocturnal animals see the same things that we see, but they are able to observe them longer and in more detail. I think that the Catholic imagination asks us to see with eyes that are expanded, hopeful, and penetrating. The wonderings of medieval theologians fall under this spiritual practice, as do the apparitions of the Virgin Mary and the even more unusual and miraculous happenings, such as stigmata and healing, that come from the prayers of saints. For most of us, our eyes are too small. We miss too much.

The world is all wrapped up with God; both the good and the bad, hurricanes and fair autumn sunshine, the Haitian poor and the entitled rich, spiritual doubt and religious certainty; it is all One Mystery. And Catholics can see with this sort of detail and complexity. This is why Graham Greene said to a reporter at the end of his life, when asked what his Catholic faith ultimately meant to him, "It's a mystery which can't be destroyed . . . even by the Church."[17]

But It's Too Easy

"Oh, I know what you think. You think my God is an illusion like the windmills [of Don Quixote]. But He exists, I tell you, I don't just believe in Him. I touch Him."

—GRAHAM GREENE, *MONSIGNOR QUIXOTE*[18]

Before the Resurrection, the followers of Jesus were almost exclusively Jewish. Aside from the centurion in Capernaum (Luke 7), we know little of Gentiles who recognized Jesus for who he really was. In the eventful final week of the Passion, though, the Gospels and tradition tell of at least two more Gentiles who became convinced that Jesus was the real deal, the Son of God: Dismas the Good Thief, who asked Jesus while dying beside him, "Remember me when you come into your kingdom," and Procula, the wife of Pilate, who warned her husband not to condemn Jesus to death.

After the Resurrection and Ascension, things must have gotten crazy. The disciples scattered all around the Roman Empire, spreading the news, preaching, and establishing the first small groups that eventually began to resemble churches.

They gathered quietly and often lived in community together. Their religion was viewed, by themselves and others, as a type of reformed Judaism. They preached Jesus as the Messiah ("anointed one" in Hebrew), the Christ ("anointed one" in Greek), and within thirty or so years were being called "Christians." Most of the church groups dispensed with mandatory Jewish rituals for new Christians, and they realized that their faith was actually something quite new. For Christians, there was no Mount Sinai, where God would deliver on tablets what is and is not important; it was up to the people to figure that out. What was most important was the kingdom of God, which Jesus said was here and now and which became the life and work of all those who followed Christ despite the dangers and despite their whereabouts, scattered about the Mediterranean world.

For 250 years, Christians remained a tiny minority of the Roman Empire, persecuted for most of that time. They endured purges of martyrdom under emperors who were unnerved by the sect's lack of reverence for the Roman gods. Some Christians settled in cities throughout Asia Minor and beyond, while others hid in the catacombs beneath Rome. They circulated the stories of Jesus, his Blessed Mother, the miracles, and the teachings of the Gospels, and they settled into commemorating the birth, teachings, sacrifice, and Resurrection of Christ as the central purpose of their lives. Then suddenly, in October of the year 312, the Roman Emperor Constantine saw a vision.

Before facing his rival, Maxentius, on the Milvian Bridge spanning the Tiber River into Rome, Constantine prayed (or at least claimed to have prayed) to the God of Christianity for victory in battle. Constantine dreaded facing Maxentius and his fierce armies. Maxentius was adept in the magical arts, and Constantine—who was himself devoted to a variety of gods—decided to pray to the "Supreme God," the God of Abraham, Isaac, Jacob, and Jesus, the God who had been so beautifully witnessed in the lives of the Christian martyrs in the amphitheaters at the hands of earlier emperors.

On October 27, the day before the battle, Constantine prayed and said that he had a vision of the cross in the sun. Later that evening, Constantine said that Christ Himself had appeared to him in a dream and commanded him to use the chi-rho sign, a symbol that features the first two Greek letters of the name Christ, "as a safeguard" in battle. "Conquer by this!" Constantine said he was told by God.

And so Constantine outfitted his soldiers with the symbol of Christ, and they conquered Maxentius, attributing their victory to God Almighty. The following year, after Constantine had become the undisputed leader of the western half of the Roman Empire, he passed the Edict of Milan and eliminated the prejudice against Christianity. Thus began what is called the "Peace of the Church," when Christians went from being a persecuted minority to being the only kind of citizen in just a few decades.

That may have been the worst thing that could have happened to Christian faith—becoming mainstream, preferred, easy, no longer marginal. The Milvian Bridge led to institutionalized Christianity. It led, in fact, to what we now call Christendom, with all of its ceremony, pomp, hierarchy, and disputes about hierarchy. The first "holy fools" of Christian history originated in the century after Constantine, challenging the all-too-sensible approach that Christians soon took to accommodating this world. These fools modeled themselves after the foolishness of Christ; they made themselves fools—often doing counterintuitive and outwardly outrageous things in order to stick their finger in the collective eye of institutionalized faith. In later centuries, when Christianity once again came under political pressure and Christian lives were threatened, whether by Arab invasions in Europe during the Middle Ages or Communist revolutions in Russia in the twentieth century, holy fools became less common, almost unnecessary.

Constantine ushered in the era of building wealth and power and influence—and losing in the process some of the beautiful aspects of ancient faith. We still live today in the shadow of the Milvian Bridge in our claiming God's favor as well as in the relative ease with which we live our faith.

The institutional church began at the Milvian Bridge, for both good and ill. Faith became easy, compared to what it had been like in the first few centuries. But the security of knowing your life would not be in danger for living as a Christian also brought enormous benefits. Theologians and poets had time and freedom to soar in their praise and contemplation of Christ. The practices of the sacraments and the development of sacramentals (to be discussed shortly) brought beauty and meaning to a life lived within the walls of the church.

Within a generation of Constantine's vision and victory in 312, the new bishop of Jerusalem, Cyril, wrote a treatise in which he for the first time differentiated what was the *Catholic Church*. Cyril was distinguishing between orthodoxy and early heretical groups that were popping up around the Roman Empire—groups such as the Montanists, followers of Montanus, who believed he could prophesy with the power of the Holy Spirit; they also believed that a person who had committed a serious sin after conversion could likely never be truly redeemed.

Here is what Cyril wrote:

> And if ever you are sojourning in cities, inquire not simply where the Lord's House is (for the other sects of the profane also attempt to call their own dens houses

> of the Lord), nor merely where the Church is, but where is the Catholic Church. For this is the peculiar name of this Holy Church, the mother of us all, which is the spouse of our Lord Jesus Christ, the Only-begotten Son of God . . . and is a figure and copy of Jerusalem which is above, which is free, and the mother of us all; which before was barren, but now has many children. . . . In this Holy Catholic Church receiving instruction and behaving ourselves virtuously, we shall attain the kingdom of heaven, and inherit *eternal life;* for which also we endure all toils, that we may be made partakers thereof from the Lord.[19]

Earlier in that treatise, Cyril explained, "It is called Catholic, then, because it extends over all the world, from one end of the earth to the other; and because it teaches universally and completely one and all the doctrines which ought to come to human knowledge, concerning things both visible and invisible, heavenly and earthly." The Catholic Church became the mother of the faithful in those centuries of late antiquity.

The same feeling extended and deepened in the Middle Ages. As noted earlier, *Catholic* means "universal." To be Catholic means to practice spirituality in ways that have been universally understood since the earliest days: We are most Catholic when we are most inclusively Christian. For instance, when we pray the common liturgical prayers of the Daily Office, come together to comfort each other, care for the less fortunate, reconcile enemies and create friendships, praise and participate in the mystery of the Risen Christ, we are both ancient and Catholic.

But Catholic also means more than universal. Ignatius of Antioch wrote around the year 110 that "wherever Jesus

Christ is, there is the Catholic Church." He was making a distinction between Judaism and this new movement known as Christianity. *Places* were no longer the primary expression of God (the Temple or the city of Jerusalem). Instead, God was to be found in a *person,* a unique combination of God and man. Jesus said that he would be present wherever two or more people are together in his name. The Apostle Paul, who was the first Christian mystic, instructed first-century believers how to die in Christ, rise in Christ, achieve fellowship with Christ, belong to Christ, be laid hold of by Christ, embrace Christ, and be in Christ. The space between us is holy just as the Christ inside of us is holy. For those who remain outside of the institutional church—for whatever reasons—there is still an ocean of Catholic life and practice open to you. One can be *almost*, while still being *essentially,* Catholic.

So that is why living out our faith is tougher because of the Milvian Bridge—because it is relatively easy compared to what it was like for the first Christians. The tradition remained diverse for several hundred years after Constantine, but over time, the bishop in Rome took on greater and greater authority. The Roman Curia, or religious government, became larger, and by the later Middle Ages, its bureaucracy and the pope were ruling in the same way that kings and their courts ruled in the secular world. Corruption and other problems creep in whenever an institution gets large, and it is those aspects of the story that unfortunately tend to receive all of the coverage today. But the same institution that began to solidify in the fourth century and grew to wield power also enthralled the minds and spirits of poets, philosophers, painters, and fishermen.

Taking Vows

> The sacred exists and is stronger than all our rebellions.
>
> —Czeslaw Milosz, *Visions from San Francisco Bay*[20]

I know this is true. My own life has been full of rebellions—small ones, for the most part—and I always come back to the reminders that God is here. Faith seems to require only one thing: moments, at least, when we abandon our egos; times when we listen to the ground of our being and discover it, even fleetingly, in God.

John Henry Newman, the famous nineteenth-century convert from Anglicanism to Catholicism, compared belief to trust, an argument that has convinced many people ever since. Mentioning one difficult doctrine—that Christ is physically present in the consecrated body and blood of the Eucharistic host and wine—Newman says, "It is difficult, impossible to imagine, I grant—but how is it difficult to believe?"[21]

Swallow your doubts, and will yourself to believe, right? But that isn't what Newman was saying. Instead he appeals to tradition—the oldest, most Catholic way of knowing. "I had no difficulty in believing it as soon as I believed that the Catholic Roman Church was the oracle of God, and that she had declared this doctrine to be part of the original revelation."[22] This is the trusting retreat that religious people sometimes make to answer challenges for evidence. It is as if to turn the tables on the one who doubts and say, look at the past two thousand years and tell me why you would *not* believe something so beautiful and so necessary for millions of others.

A famous Catholic thinker of the seventeenth century, Blaise Pascal, once said that knowing God and loving God are two very different things. Nothing could be further from the truth, in my experience. Pascal was a philosopher; in contrast, monastic spirituality teaches us how it is God's nature only to be known with love. In fact, the deeper we love, and the more that we come to understand God with the heart, the more likely we are to know something about God. Loving, hoping, desiring—these are the things the poets and hymn writers have sung about for centuries, because they are the essence of knowledge of divine things. With King David, we may ask of God, "Incline my heart unto thy testimonies" (Psalm 119:36). In other words, turn my heart to believe more. That's how it works.

And these are the reasons why we take vows—because we love, desire, and hope—and because we believe that these cravings have Divine origins. More than fifteen hundred years ago, Saint Augustine wrote in the first spiritual autobiography ever written (the *Confessions*) that his heart was restless until it found its home in God. That is the beginning of a vow, the perfect example of what drives us to vow-taking.

The *Catholic Encyclopedia* is unforgiving on the definition of a vow: "A vow is defined as a promise made to God.

The promise is binding, and so differs from a simple resolution, which is a present purpose to do or omit certain things in the future."[23] Put another way, our words have power. Words are like actions: they *do* things. When we speak the words of a vow, we believe that we are taking action with those words. To say "I will always love and care for you" is to do it, right then. But of course, a vow must be fulfilled, carried out. Vow-taking means little to most people today, but Catholics take vows and, it is hoped, stick by them. Most people avoid taking them, and if they do take one, it is done with an understanding that the words have no power. But that is not the way it is supposed to be.

There are many types of vows. Some are made publicly, to be recognized by others—such as baptismal vows in church—while others are made privately and personally—such as a commitment to God to do or not to do something.

There are also vows taken that involve giving up one's rights or surrendering rights to another. These are vows taken to enter religious orders, for instance. These are called "solemn" vows and usually involve promising things like obedience to a superior or sharing one's property and livelihood or chastity—all for the sake of joining a religious group. Francis of Assisi took what was for him a solemn vow of voluntary poverty; he made it to God alone until others came and joined him, making the same vow to God and to each other.

Vows are not exclusive to Christianity. People of many religious traditions follow rules that are very much like our vow-taking. A vow is a promise to obey, either another person or a rule of life. We could learn a lot from our Jewish friends, for instance, who often realize that the rules of their childhoods are good after all. I have known many Jews who grew up in Orthodox homes with rules to eat kosher and pray the Kaddish (mourner's prayer) and keep the Sabbath, stopped doing those things when they became adults, only to return to them later in life. As it turns out, eating kosher and grieving well and observing the Sabbath are all good for you!

What sort of vows have you taken? Baptismal? Marriage? Have you ever made a vow to one of your children? I have taken all of these, and I would never violate them. Some people also make vows to a particular place; in monastic parlance, this is called a "vow of stability." A monk promises never to leave, which is like promising always to work things out. Do you remember that feeling—perhaps from your adolescence—of storming out of the room when you were upset? You can't do that anymore—not if you make a vow to a spouse, partner, or place.

You don't have to be a monk or a nun to take a vow of stability. Many people where I live in Vermont, for instance, take another form of these vows that might better be described as the vow of stewardship, promising to care for the piece of earth on which they live. The sustainable living movement is gaining steam around the globe, and people are taking more of these sorts of vows.

The vow of obedience interests me most of all. It is a solemn vow for committed monastics. But what is its relevance for me? I have had spiritual directors to whom I vowed a certain form of obedience. I wouldn't have jumped off a cliff for them, but I did do what they told me to do, to try and deepen my spiritual life. I've also always seen my marriage vows to be similar to obedience; I think that we vowed to obey each other.

But how is it possible to be obedient to others and yet still be individual, critical, reasoning? This is where the Protestant and Catholic imaginations collide. The modern self was born with the protests of Martin Luther against the late medieval Catholic Church. The word *egocentrism* didn't exist before Luther's sixteenth century. Democracy was born there as well. One of the pillars of the Reformation was the notion of the "priesthood of all believers." The phrase originated in 1 Peter 2:4, 7–9:

> Come to him, a living stone, though rejected by mortals yet chosen and precious in God's sight, and like living stones, let yourselves be built into a spiritual house, to be a holy priesthood, to offer spiritual sacrifices acceptable to God through Jesus Christ. For it stands in scripture: "See, I am laying in Zion a stone, a cornerstone chosen and precious; and whoever believes in him will not be put to shame." To you then who believe, he is precious. . . . You are a chosen race, a royal priesthood, a holy nation, God's own people, in order that you may proclaim the mighty acts of him who called you out of darkness into his marvellous light.

The Lollards—an English political and religious reform movement in the fourteenth and fifteenth centuries—were the first group to begin focusing on this passage, emphasizing that the new covenant of Christ intends to create priests of all believers. Just as the priests of ancient Israel once entered the Holy of Holies of the Temple to offer sacrifices for the sins of the people, the earliest Protestants believed that Catholic priests had made their own role into a necessity when in fact it wasn't. Each person may make this sort of priestly approach to God, without fear.

In the early sixteenth century in Germany, Martin Luther picked up on the idea. He taught that everyone who believes in Christ is a priest—the "priesthood of all believers." He wrote and spoke often of the ways in which

Christians become full participants in the work of God, equal to each other in every respect—"shaking off the yoke of tyranny," a common phrase of his that referred to popes, priests, monks, nuns—knowing that we who have Christ have all things that are Christ's and can do all things that once were thought to belong only to priests.

Before Luther found the chutzpah to speak up boldly against the Roman Church, people did what they were told. In fact, as the young British theologian Theo Hobson recently noted, "Secularism was a Protestant invention."[24] Before Luther, you didn't have the choice but to be religious, to be Catholic.

A true Catholic will desire improvement and reform, but not at the expense of unity. "Luther's self becomes practically the centre of gravity of everything," wrote Jacques Maritain.[25] The human self replaced the Church as the chief arbiter of what is good, and true. We still live in the era of Luther, and we usually think of what he did as positive. It was positive, of course, in many ways, and there is surely no turning back.

We still take vows, and we still decide to believe things that we don't have the reasons for. Two centuries after Luther, the European Enlightenment continued the process of separating reason from truth. Philosophers like Descartes and Rousseau broke the stranglehold that the medieval system of Thomas Aquinas had held on human life and thought for more than half a millennium. Until only recently, ethics, physics, and metaphysics were all wrapped up together. One looked to a theological system for knowledge of most anything.

Saint Bernard of Clairvaux said in his first sermon on the Song of Songs: "Only the touch of the Holy Spirit can inspire a song like this, and only personal experience can unfold its meaning. Those who are experienced in the mystery may revel in it; all others should burn with desire to attain to it rather than merely settle for learning about it."[26]

While it is easy to criticize statements such as Bernard's as anti-intellectual, they are compelling to those who do more than dip their toe in the water of religious experience, finding that there is something to this logic after all.

The early-twentieth-century poet and mystic, Raïssa Maritain once wrote admiringly about the Jewish philosopher Baruch Spinoza because his writings urged human beings "to love God intellectually, without asking to be loved in return." There is something tremendously appealing about this sort of purity. Many a Protestant has converted to Catholicism in order to reach this sort of simplicity and purity of obedience.

The vow of obedience is—like any understanding of God—contained in love and devotion. The Catholic worldview appeals to the pure intellect in ways that are different from and more embodied than dissenting traditions. Catholic belief is inseparable from spiritual practice with feet, hands, sinew and muscle, lips, and heart, as well as head. It eschews the empiricism and materialism of Enlightenment ways of knowing. The ideas of faith are formed in us by the experiences of faith. The heart and lips can teach us enough to fill libraries, but the brain alone will only fill books.

Czeslaw Milosz wrote often about the ways that the people of the twentieth century are seemingly "wandering among ruins." The ruins are the old ways and traditions, the old systems of thought, including those times when the taking of vows seemed more necessary. Writing during the German occupation of Poland in World War II, Milosz struggled to reconcile a religious worldview with the problems of life. In place of such a worldview, he reflected in a letter to a friend on "the existence of that great expanse of darkness that surrounds us, that spreads out not only beyond us but inside us, too."[27] His life's work was an attempt to penetrate that darkness with spiritual light that was relevant, eternal, and Catholic.

There is wisdom, harmony, and interconnectedness in the Catholic worldview—a sort of stubborn refusal to accept the dissolution of the unity of belief and practice from the ancient and medieval Church—that millions of people today find more compelling and true than wandering in the ruins. The *Catechism of the Catholic Church* says, "A vow is an act of devotion in which the Christian dedicates himself to God or promises him some good work. By fulfilling his vows he renders to God what has been promised and consecrated to Him" (para. 2102). There is a stubbornness to vow-taking and vow-keeping.

Becoming a Saint

I became aware that I, as an individual believer, stood in a very long and august lineage of the faithful, stretching back to the apostles and Church Fathers. The picture had changed for me: it was no longer primarily me, my Bible, and Jesus (although heaven knows that is not altogether a bad picture: the only question is, is it the *whole* picture?).

—Thomas Howard, *Lead, Kindly Light*[28]

Catherine Benencasa was born in 1347 in Siena, Italy, the twenty-third of twenty-five children. Like other great saints before her—such as Saint Clare of Assisi or Saint Lucia—Catherine's parents misunderstood her love for God and urged her to accept a husband, as all good girls were supposed to do. They pressured her to the point where Catherine rebelled. Now some might not call it rebellion—because of her holy intent—but it was. Still a young girl, she sheared her own hair as a way of tonsuring herself for a religious life. She was determined never to wed and instead to spend her life in prayer and contemplation, service to others, and teaching. She disobeyed and disappointed her parents while starting on the path to becoming one of the most beloved saints of the Church.

Catherine's letters are warm and full of theological teaching, often offered to those in authority from one who was untrained. She used the colloquial Italian word *Babbo* to address the pope, showing her affection for him as a person and as her spiritual father. Pope Pius II officially canonized Saint Catherine of Siena in 1461, eighty years after her death, and Pope Paul VI made her the first woman "Doctor" of the Church in 1970, signaling the importance of her writings for theological understanding.

Saints are made by the Roman Catholic Church in complicated ways, with minutiae of detail and argument, usually the result of many years of investigation and hearings that resemble courtrooms, but with a rationale that every non-Catholic Christian can easily understand: A saint is a person who has died and is now certainly in heaven. Therefore, you may confidently ask that person, in prayer, to advocate for, comfort, and inspire you on your own spiritual journey.

Every Christian is supposed to desire sainthood. Dorothy Day once famously replied to a reporter who asked if she hoped to be canonized one day, "Don't dismiss me that easily!" She was referring to the way that the canonized often led to plastic statues but not living exemplars. Saints matter—not so much because their images are printed on to little cards with prayers on the back but because they are among us, as we live into eternity with that cloud of witnesses that the book of Hebrews speaks about.

We are supposed to be supported by the saints who have gone before us and then to desire sainthood for ourselves. One of the best parts about living like a saint is that it explains why you are often misunderstood by others.

Saints are supposed to be misunderstood. History is replete with examples of parents and siblings—often even Christian ones—trying to persuade loved ones not to follow a path that leads to sainthood. Many people don't understand why someone would take faith so seriously as to want to become a saint. They don't know why you would want less money, influence, or pleasure by choosing a more spiritual life. You may have heard "Don't you want to be happy?" as an argument against what you have in mind for your life. I have known teenagers who did not feel at home with their families. This wasn't because they were abused or neglected, rebellious or unloved, but because their spiritual motives were misunderstood.

Like Catherine of Siena, no follower of Christ can escape the perception that he or she is somehow odd or mistaken or naive. Like Moses, we are strangers living in a strange land. But we do it together, and that's why the communion of saints is so important; we don't stand before God alone; we support each other.

You have saints around you right now. Teilhard de Chardin once prayed, "I call before me the whole vast anonymous army of living humanity; those who surround me and support me though I do not know them."[29] We are *all* in this for the long haul.

The sainthood we desire is something that we first enter into upon Baptism. We become children of God—and then we walk the path of growing into that inheritance. Eventually, we encounter that teaching of Jesus that says, "Be perfect as I am perfect." I often wonder how many a person has dropped the faith thing altogether because of that bit of advice.

It is no accident that a majority of those who have been canonized as saints over the centuries have come from religious orders. The monastic tradition, more than any other, teaches us that being a saint is not about being perfect but rather about following those who have come before. It is about being faithful to your spiritual practice and having a mind illumined by faith. From the Desert Fathers and Mothers of the early centuries to Saint Benedict, who wrote the fundamental rules for monastic life, to Saint Francis of Assisi and Saint Francis de Sales and the modern-era saints Thérèse of Lisieux, Katharine Drexel, and others—they all show how it is possible to come to the sweetness of an unutterable love in Christ when we are obedient, listen, and follow.

My friend Basil Pennington used to say that striving toward something is a way of obtaining it. We are what we strive to be, and we are where we strive to be. Heaven happens now, just as hell does. Catholic spirituality is full of saints and of talk about becoming saints because that is precisely what life is about. That's why sainthood is not supposed to be all that unusual; it is ordinary, human, and full of frailty, but it is our conscious attempt to live in our true self, without blinders and without deceptions.

Becoming saints, we do very personal and interpersonal work. We help others toward conversion by helping them figure out who they are and how to strip their false selves and uncover their true selves. But saintliness is not all about an inward glow or satisfaction. Not at all. As Saint Paul said, it would all be meaningless without love for others. "Though I command languages both human and angelic—if I speak without love, I am no more than a gong booming or a cymbal clashing" (1 Corinthians 13:1). That is exactly what saints do every day. In recent history, the names of Martin Luther King Jr., Oscar Romero, and Desmond Tutu leap to mind. In the present day, Archbishop Pius Ncube of Zimbabwe is one of the profound examples of a saint speaking with love and courage, as he has been urging the people of his country to make nonviolent resistance in order to overthrow a military dictatorship.

The priorities of outward-looking sainthood are endless. "Love never comes to an end. But if there are prophecies, they will be done away with; if tongues, they will fall silent; and if knowledge, it will be done away with" (1 Corinthians 13:8). What is more important than building and gilding churches? Reducing poverty by looking at our financial resources as not our own. What is better than protecting ourselves from those who threaten us? Caring properly for the millions who sit in prisons. Reducing the number of abortions by supporting contraception education. Speaking out against religious discrimination wherever it occurs.

Like the Buddhist bodhisattva who waits for the ultimate enlightenment until he has helped others find their way down the right path, Catholics do likewise. This often means that we understand what it means to sin, be forgiven, and grow into a new place with God. The three-step ladder of sin, forgiveness, and beginning again is lost on many of the people around us. In fact, those are words easily said but less easily understood. We might want to occasionally slow down as we say them, but it is more important that we add to the witness of our lives those activities and desires that make an environment where the words make sense.

Saints also develop lively relationships with God. I read recently that studies have shown that people who do not use their bodies much—who live mostly "in their heads"—actually regress emotionally. Their emotional responses are fewer and less keen than those of people who use their bodies actively. The same is true of us, which is why those

Catholic pieties that some people scoff at and others have long ago abandoned are being rediscovered by people of all backgrounds. Kneeling, making the sign of the cross, praying the rosary, walking on even a short pilgrimage, allowing someone to wash your feet on Maundy Thursday, devouring the Eucharistic host and wine—these are not just spiritual (by which, we often think, "in our heads") but also physical actions that somehow release synapses of connection to the Divine in our lives.

As saints, we also listen very carefully, and we sense what is happening in our lives and in the lives of those around us. I'm no advocate of the fortune-teller, but I do believe there are times when another Christian may know what is happening to me before I do. I have had friends tell me that they began praying for me before I even asked for it because they knew that something was wrong. I also believe that the earliest stories of Saint Francis of Assisi and the animals (and other saints with similar tales) are for the most part true. He spoke to birds who listened attentively; he counseled with a wolf and a raven; he showed a gentleness with species of creation that is both unusual and natural. Catholics can learn to see and make connections between creatures and species in ways that are easily disbelieved by others. This skill grows out of a life full of the Spirit of God, sensitive to the incarnate nature of faith, in those who learn to listen and be quiet.

Finally, saints love life because this is where heaven begins. Saint Catherine of Siena used to say, "All the way to heaven is heaven." The journey of being human is the same journey as being a child of God. But this doesn't mean that we always look around ourselves and feel at home. As Teilhard de Chardin once prayed, "All of us, Lord, from the moment we are born feel within us this disturbing mixture of remoteness and nearness."[30] We sometimes feel at home because despite our circumstances, we are surrounded by other saints, that cloud of witnesses, and we are indwelt by a God who knows precisely what it means to be lonely, unwanted, despairing.

Becoming a saint is just as vital for those living faith outside church walls as it is for those of us inside. If you find your spirituality completely outside the organized church, you have probably been struck by the irony of belief versus practice in churches today. In Catholic churches, for instance, the difference can be confusing for those on the outside looking in. From the pope to the parish pew in Peoria, lots of Roman Catholics disregard whole swaths of official theology and practical teaching yet still hold passionately to the traditions of being Catholic. The same devout people who are at early weekday morning Mass may disregard the pope's latest official teaching on sexual morality. How is that possible, and what does that mean?

The same is hardly ever true of Protestants. To be Lutheran, for instance, is pretty much to accept the entire spoonful of theology, teaching, and tradition. If you change your mind, you most likely change your denomination. So what's different about being Catholic, as opposed to being Protestant, that makes ambivalence seem more natural? Basically this: you realize that you're in it for life. To be Catholic is to know that you are in this for the long haul. To be almost Catholic does not mean being easy Catholic. Catholic always means a lifetime, like marriage, paying taxes, or pain. Just as you may *become* some brand or other of Protestant, you are always *becoming* a Catholic.

SECTION THREE

FAITH WITH FLESH

He Loved His Own Flesh

> Our birth He reforms from death by a second birth from heaven; our flesh He restores from every harassing malady; when leprous, He cleanses it of the stain; when blind, He rekindles its light; when palsied, He renews its strength; when possessed with devils, He exorcises it; when dead, He reanimates it,—then shall *we* blush to own it?
>
> —TERTULLIAN, *ON THE FLESH OF CHRIST*

One of the earliest apologists for Christianity, Tertullian defended the faith against heretics who denied that Jesus was really a man. These intellectual opponents (Marcion was the primary one) believed that Jesus was ghostlike and that his flesh was literally unreal. He couldn't be both God and man because flesh would sully God, they thought. "He loved his own flesh," Tertullian says at one point in his argument. Not a phrase that you've probably ever seen before, I realize, but it is true: Jesus loved his body. That's an enormous piece of understanding what it means for God to become human. But we don't hear it. Perhaps we *can't* hear it anymore.

> An angel of the Lord stood over them and the glory of the Lord shone round them. They were terrified, but the angel said, "Do not be afraid. Look, I bring you news of great joy, a joy to be shared by the whole people. Today in the town of David a Savior has been born to you; he is Christ the Lord. And here is a sign for you: you will find a baby wrapped in swaddling clothes and lying in a manger" [Luke 2:9–12].

In the popular imagination when we hear this story, we see only an adorable baby in a manger. The Nativity story has been sentimentalized so much as to lose the meaning of Christ as a temporal, fleshy human. In truth, that's how God changed everything, and so much of Catholic spiritual practice flows from this reality.

Even the legend of the stars aligning on the eve of the Nativity has perpetuated the myths—rather than the essence—of incarnation and obscured the wonder and strangeness of it. Magi from the East track the planets and follow them in the night sky to Jerusalem and on to Bethlehem. We're still looking up—which is precisely what was supposed to end in that stable. Instead, we look down to see Christ the infant. As Tertullian inveighed eighteen hundred years ago against Marcion, "Of course you are horrified also at the infant, which is shed into life with the embarrassments which accompany it from the womb; you likewise, of course, loathe it even after it is washed." He became one of us, born into a messy, complicated, human life. Catholic spirituality has known as much for at least those eighteen hundred years.

The carnality of faith scares us and always has. The tendency has always been to either deny it, which leads to heresy, or explain it in metaphysical terms, which leads to theology. For nearly two millennia, theologians have wanted to sanctify or sanitize all of this mess. The often bizarre story of "original sin" was told in order to explain Christ the creature in more divine, metaphysical, terms. The theory goes something like this: Our physical and spiritual parents, Adam and Eve, committed the first sin against God in the Garden of Eden when they ate of the forbidden fruit. Somehow, that sin was then transmitted from parent to child ever since Adam and Eve and their first children. Some say that it is the father's semen that contains the stain of sin; others have said that the mother's womb carries it. Regardless, as the theory goes, each person is guilty of sin, "original" sin, from the moment we are born, and it comes about as a result of sex and birth and the stain we can never remove from our bodies.

According to the theory, you can't escape original sin. If you've been born, you've been born with it already attached to you. And it does not really have anything to do with actual sinning. It would be difficult to deny the reality of universal, actual, sin—but original sin feels like one of those myths used to explain things away. In this case, it dims the light on the humanness of Jesus, making him human but only for a grand, metaphysical reason—to become the first and only human to be born without sin.

Enter the sacrificial blood of Jesus and the necessity of the "atonement," as it is called. Just as something in the human body is said to pass original sin from one person to the next, so did the theologians unite other bodily fluids with our salvation from that condition. Original sin attempts to explain why Christ had to become incarnate as a man, suffer, and die in order to *atone* for our sins. Saint Paul's metaphor of Jesus as the "Passover Lamb" is very apt, according to this view. Jesus was a substitution sacrifice for our sins. You may have heard this in Sunday school: Jesus is supposed to have metaphysically taken our sins upon himself—hence the angry darkness on Calvary when, in the last moments, Jesus cried out to the Father, "My God, my God, why have you forsaken me?" He then cried out again "in a loud voice" and "yielded up his spirit. And suddenly, the veil of the Sanctuary was torn in two from top to bottom, the earth quaked, the rocks were split, the tombs opened and the bodies of many holy people rose from the dead" (Matthew 27:46–52). He thus became the ultimate atonement for all sin. Medieval theologians like Anselm of Canterbury and Thomas Aquinas believed that this was the best way to explain verses such as 1 Corinthians 15:22. "Just as all die in Adam, so in Christ all will be brought to life."

And here's where the odd beliefs about bodily fluids enter back in: The theory of atonement was said to be necessary not because of actual sin in the lives of people but because of original or inherited sin. If semen or the birth canal passes sin from one human to the next, then it was believed to be blood (Jesus' blood) that would fix it, making it possible to break the cycle.

The flesh of Christ is far better than all of that. Jesus was born as one of us because God loves us without measure, and God wanted to do whatever was necessary to be in relationship with us in ways we can hardly imagine. Jesus did not die to satisfy a debt or as a surrogate sacrifice for our collective sins inherited from the first parents. That explanation seems to imply that God had a sort of blood lust, seeking the suffering of anyone—even His own Son—to satisfy Divine wrath and justice. Instead, God sets prisoners free. God comes to dwell in us. That's what the work of Christ on the cross means, and the work of God, through Christ, today. That human Jesus—that oh so human Jesus—is whom we love when we look with our senses to Christ.

All of Catholic spiritual practice flows from this. A Catholic life is about recognizing and honoring as sacred the multitude of tangible and tactile connections in our lives. In other words, we almost have to redefine the word *spiritual* because we often misunderstand it. Spiritual is not in opposition to earthly or physical. Our spiritual lives are simply our lives, including everything we do, touch, sense, and express. We aren't supposed to set out to do "spiritual" things or to "be spiritual." That's not how it works.

Every moment of human life is full of opportunity to know God, which is very different from trying to be spiritual all the time. Brother Lawrence, a seventeenth-century Carmelite monk, talked about this in *The Practice of the Presence of God*. For Brother Lawrence, daily moments of work and duty and manual labor were filled with God's presence. Whether he was washing the dishes in the abbey kitchen or cobbling shoes for his brothers, he found delight in doing what he called "little things for God." He learned to turn his heart genuinely to joy at the smallest and meanest tasks.

But Brother Lawrence's way is only a small piece of what it means to tap into the carnality of faith. Brother Lawrence achieved his joy in physical work by practicing what a Buddhist might call "disinterestedness." *The Practice of the Presence of God* says that "he did not remember the things he did, and was almost unaware even when he was occupied in doing them. On leaving the table he did not know what he had eaten."[1] And so on. This reminds me of the story about the Baal Shem Tov—the founder of the Hasidic movement—intended to illustrate the true meaning of fasting: the great rebbe simply forgot to eat for a few days while in a mystical trance.

The carnality of faith is much more than living disinterestedly in matters of matter. We are to be interested and attentive, seeking and seeing, how our human lives are extensions of Christ. To love our flesh as Jesus loved his own is to fill the physical events, stuff, interactions of life with spiritual meaning because they are indeed full of meaning. We can wash the dishes, repair shoes, prepare and eat a feast, and love doing those things—not because we've turned our mind elsewhere but because Christ showed us that physical life is marvelous.

The Sensuousness of Jesus

> What she didn't understand, she being spiritual and seeing religion as spirit, was that it took religion to save me from the spirit world, from orbiting the earth like Lucifer and the angels, that it took nothing less than touching the thread off the misty interstates and eating Christ himself to make me mortal man again and let me inhabit my own flesh and love her in the morning.
>
> —Walker Percy, *Love in the Ruins*[2]

There is a difference between being *sensuous* and *sensual.* In his human nature, Jesus surely experienced both, but my experience of Jesus is entirely of the first sort.

To be sensuous is to be readily affected by and through one's senses. A sensuous person is alive to the knowledge and imagination and information that comes through the five senses. To be sensual, in contrast, is to incline toward gratifying, arousing, or exciting one's senses or appetites. From *sensual* comes *sensuality*—referring to what we might call "animal instincts," or those appetites that are "lower" than reason.

John Milton appears to have been the first person to coin the word *sensuous* to distinguish from the titillation of the *sensual*. He once explained that the soul and the body are "sensuous colleagues" when joined together in a human being. Samuel Taylor Coleridge, another poet, took up the distinction and later declared, "The understanding, wherever it does not possess or use the reason, as another and inward eye, may be defined the conception of the sensuous."[3] And Jack Kerouac, a much later poet, wrote in one of his "psalm-meditations," "Thank you, O Lord, for small meeds of truth and warmth Thou hast poured into this willing vessel, and thank you for confusion, mistake, and Horror's sadness, that breed in Thy Name. Keep my flesh in Thee everlasting."[4]

You could say that the entire purpose of God in Christ was sensuous. The classic painters understood this: so many of their greatest works show a Jesus who is clearly sensuous. Christ is God with us, which is sensuous through and through: in our birthing, ailing, healing, sex, hunger, and even dying. Christ is God deciding to be so with us that God becomes one of us. Our experience of faith is full of the sensuous, as his was.

My life has been enriched most by the sensuous ways of Catholic spirituality. Flannery O'Connor once observed, "The things we see, hear, smell and touch affect us long before we believe anything at all."[5] We touch by fingering our rosary beads, by feeling holy water on our fingertips and chrism oil and ashes on the forehead at Baptism, at Confirmation, and on Ash Wednesday. We touch hands and sometimes lips when we pass the peace. We touch our knees to the floor at the Mass as the account of the Last Supper is recited.

We sweat and tremble when we are terrified. We pray, even when words don't come. We feel lonely.

We smell the sweet incense of shared worship and the home cooking of being together with friends. Whether at home or in the pews, we pray from Psalm 141: "Yahweh, I am calling, hurry to me, listen to my voice when I call to you. May my prayer be like incense in your presence." But we also cannot help, at times, smelling the person sitting next to us. Both smells are important in knowing that Christ is there.

We hear the Word of the Lord as it is read by our friends from the lectern, as well as when they counsel us in difficult times. We listen to medieval chant of the Word as well. The sound of music fills the halls of our churches and our MP3 players, and whatever sort of music it is, it can lead us to God. We also hear the Angelus bells of our lives—which once called monastic communities each day to pray to the Virgin Mary—and they return us again and again through sound to her, who always points us to God.

We taste the host on the tongue. The casseroles at parish suppers and family get-togethers. The wine and delicious, gluttonous foods on Shrove Tuesday. We taste our arid tongues on days of fasting, and we yearn for something more sumptuous.

Above all, we see. We work to train our sight to see what is, as well as what can be. Saint Anselm, the philosopher, once said that there are three ways of knowing. In the first way, we have thoughts in our brains that imagine what could happen in the physical world. This happens, for example, if we imagine a scene that we may paint with watercolors, even though the painting does not yet exist. The second way of knowing is the completion of the first: there are times when we have thoughts in our brains that match the world in front of us. The ideas we had about painting a scene become the scene that we have painted. It is the disconnected, unsatisfactory nature of these two ways of knowing that undergirds most liberal theology and is also so easily caricatured in the popular atheism of people like Ronald Dawkins and Sam Harris.

But Anselm's third way of knowing is the one that is most important. In the third way, there are realities in the world around us that are not yet captured in any meaningful way by our brains. The problem is not that there is too little of God available to our minds and senses. There is too much. God is too sensuous. We can't conceive it, sort it, ultimately grasp it. That's what trying to know God is all about. We can't do it. But we try. There's either too much information for our minds to sort and grasp, or the data are not easily absorbed. That is why the Catholic can never step entirely outside of revelation—and should never stop finding new ways to use the senses to connect with Christ.[6]

The Crucifix

> The Teddy-bear exists in order that the child may endow it with imaginary life and personality and enter into a quasi-social relationship with it. That is what "playing with it" means. . . . Too close or prolonged attention to its changeless and expressionless face impedes the play. A crucifix exists in order to direct the worshipper's thought and affections to the Passion.
>
> —C. S. Lewis, *An Experiment in Criticism*[7]

Something happened at about the time of the Protestant Reformation: the rich medieval world was gradually replaced, and the sensuousness of Christ became more and more hidden. He was no longer easily located—in the elements of the Mass, in sacred spaces, or on the crucifix. Since then, Catholics and other Christians have lost some of the faith in their senses as safe paths to feeling the mystery of God.

In the later Middle Ages, most churches had what is called a "rood screen." *Rood* is Saxon for "cross." These elaborate screens were actual dividing walls that separated the choir or chancel (where the altar was) from the nave (where the congregation was). Affixed to a rood screen would be an enormous, sculpted crucifix. Some rood screens, or portions of them, can still be seen in Catholic and Anglican churches. And Eastern Orthodox churches have a slightly different version with what is called an *iconostatis,* which is a wall in the same place that holds not only a crucifix but also an array of icons and sacred images.

Since the Reformation, both the rood screens and the sacred images once hung on them have diminished. The Protestant imagination that wants to pull the strands apart—rather than weave them together—did just that to many of the connections between the ideas and the senses of faith. Symbols, metaphors, and tangible objects were all diminished. The crucifix lost its blood as the reformers created crucifixes without the symbols of pain and suffering associated with Christ's death. The Eucharist became a bit less real as doubt crept into the mystery and miracle of bread and wine becoming transformed into body and blood. And soon the crucifix lost the very body of Jesus, and empty crosses replaced crucifixes. Faith itself—activity interpreted to be primarily of the mind—became more important as direct experience of Christ began to wane. The loss of spiritual identity our ancestors once felt on this planet can be traced back to the opening hours of the Reformation.

The loneliness of the empty cross has become one of the most potent symbols of Protestantism, for good and for ill. As G. K. Chesterton once explained, the Protestant who dismisses the dying Christ may in the end become satisfied with a dead cross. In other words, the crucifix depicts the climax of what we call Christ's Passion, and to venerate a cross without Christ on it is to lose much of its power and meaning. "To salute the Cross in that sense is literally to bow down to wood and stone," Chesterton said.[8] The salvation by faith alone preached by Martin Luther sometimes looks like a faith in faith, a way of living in the head, that replaced the Catholic understanding of the Church as the vehicle of salvation.

Saint Paul said that the cross of Christ would be a stumbling block to some and salvation to others. "Is the flesh which was crucified become as poison to the crowds in the street, or is it as a strong gladness and hope to them, as the first flower blossoming out of the earth's humus?" wondered D. H. Lawrence in *The Rainbow.*[9]

Protestant crosses replaced Catholic crucifixes long ago in an effort to emphasize the Resurrection. I remember in my own very Protestant churches as a child, we never heard sermons or lessons on the cross that did not in some way reveal the Resurrection. Whereas a Catholic would literally darken the sanctuary from the evening of Maundy Thursday until the Easter vigil service on Saturday that leads to midnight, we would preach Good Friday as if it was already Easter Sunday. The lessons of the sacrifice, the bloody lynching that was the Crucifixion, and the pain and sorrow and despair of the human Christ were lost to us. The cross by itself was for us not just incomplete but somewhat embarrassing, I think.

Protestants have the cross without the *corpus,* or body, of Jesus. These spare crosses lack the mess of the real cross of Christ. Jesus of Nazareth was a man and the second Person of the Trinity at the same time. Simone Weil once wrote in a letter to a priest—while she was arguing with him as to why she wouldn't want to be baptized into the Church—that God "is impersonal in the sense that his infinitely mysterious manner of being a Person is indefinitely different from the human manner."[10] She didn't understand just how Catholic her perspective actually was. The Catholic approach to understanding Christ accepts that his life on earth will always remain a mystery to us. The Gospels make it clear that to those who knew him, Jesus was loved like a brother but also rarely understood. It is a mystery to be experienced and felt.

I am drawn to the corpus—even the bloodiness—of the old-fashioned Roman Catholic crucifix. Not even those sanitized Jesuses hanging blithely with peace-loving eyes will do. The ancient church tried to distance themselves from the suffering of Christ; it wasn't until about the sixth century, in the early Middle Ages, that Christians felt able to take ownership of the Crucifixion. Only at that time do we see religious art and image portraying the suffering Christ.

I prefer a crucifix to a cross. I would like to see a recovery of the balance between the crucifix of Good Friday and the empty cross of Easter Sunday. Whether it is made of plaster, plastic, wood, or iron, a crucifix is not merely a metaphor; it is the symbol of the most important historical event in history: when the stuff of creation became redeemed by mixing with the stuff of God. I want to learn to be comfortable in its embarrassment as I take a symbol of a murdered man as my central image of faith. Let me know the Christ who knew what it was like to be unwanted and despised. "God's folly is wiser than human wisdom, and God's weakness is stronger than human strength" (1 Corinthians 1:25).

The Catholic journalist David Warren candidly but seriously advises fellow converts to "get a crucifix, the kind 'with the little man on it.' The kind that shows Him suffering; the kind that strikes you as rather tasteless at first, as if it might drip on your shoe. There is something peculiarly Catholic about getting a crucifix even before you go out to buy a Catholic edition of the Bible. Kneel. Cross yourself."[11] I love the last part most of all: "There is something peculiarly Catholic about getting a crucifix even before you go out to buy a Catholic edition of the Bible." Heart before head. Practice before theory. The first is always the second's best tutor.

An incarnate God is by definition messy. Mine is no Gnostic Christ, either, standing aloof and making quixotic statements. Jesus occasionally did those things, I guess, but that's not the meaning of Jesus. My Jesus was mixed up with his friends as well as his enemies, their sorrow and pain, and he bled, sweat, and cried. He drew in the dirt with his finger, prostitutes wiped his filthy feet with their hair, and he embraced the ugly and the undesirable. Such a messy, stirred-up God has lots of connections to our material world. Is it any wonder that a God who takes on our flesh—pimples, fluids, and all—should be remembered in body?

To have a crucifix in your home or around your neck is one thing, but to use it is another. There are many ways that Catholics use the crucifix in their devotions.

Most important of all, the crucifix fixes us on what is most important. That is why they are supposed to be visible. I confess that like many a Protestant, I cannot help but feel that I'm showing off in a way that Jesus said not to (go and pray in your closet) when I exhibit a crucifix. I have to get over that feeling. The Catholic whose crucifix is visible is practicing and observing faith. In fact, I think that if Christians of all backgrounds began to show expressions of their faith in public more easily, people would have more respect for our faith. Muslims who pause for public daily prayer and Jews who wear phylacteries often think that Christians are all talk and no practice.

The *Catechism of the Catholic Church* says it eloquently: "Sacred images in our churches and homes are intended to awaken and nourish our faith in the mystery of Christ. Through the icon of Christ and his works of salvation, it is he whom we adore" (para. 1192). We are supposed to adore it, meditate on it. This is why there are so many paintings of saints gazing at a crucifix hanging on the wall or holding one in hand.

The crucifix is the primary symbol of faith's mystery. The primary purpose of spirituality is to explore mysteries. These Catholic traditions connect earth and heaven. They are all part of what is called *Mysterium,* a Latin word that literally means "holy mystery." *Mysterium* is usually qualified: *Mysterium Paschale* (the mystery of Easter), *Mysterium Fidei* (the mystery of faith), *Mysterium Ecclesiae* (the mystery of the Church), and so on. Popes will often issue documents that are intended to teach the faithful about something by invoking *Mysterium.* Perhaps that is the point: always mystery.

More than anything else, *Mysterium* means the mystery of the One Incarnate Christ. Every instance of the word is essentially a reference to God in Christ. This is clearest in the classic Christmas hymn about the Nativity, "*O Magnum Mysterium*" ("O Great Mystery!"). These are all things to be experienced in ways that become almost impossible to talk meaningfully about.

One of my favorite stories from the Desert Fathers explains why I do certain spiritual practices without having all the intellectual reasons in line beforehand. A young monk approached an older, adept one and said, "Father, I am having trouble remembering the instructions that I have been given about living the spiritual life. I ask questions, I listen to the answers, and I do what is asked of me—but then I almost just as quickly forget what I've been told! What is the point to trying to learn if I am so simpleminded? Should I just give up and return to my worldly life?"

It sounds a bit like a setup to a saccharine or simple answer, doesn't it? A good occasion to say to the youngster, "Buck up! Try harder. Be diligent"—that sort of thing. But the old monk doesn't give the sort of answer one might suspect. Like a Zen master, he asks the young man to do something to discover the answer to his questions. The old man points to two empty bottles on a nearby table.

"Take two empty bottles and fill one of them completely with the oil that we use for our lamp stands. As for the other bottle, leave it empty, as it was."

The youngster did as he was told.

The old monk went on: "Now, take the full bottle and pour the oil back where it was."

The youngster did as he was told.

The old monk told him to do the same thing again—to take the same bottle that he had filled before and fill it once again with oil. And again he told him to empty the bottle. This went on for more than an hour. Methodically and patiently, the young man did as he was told.

Now it just so happened that this young novice's job in the community of monks was to clean the bottles that were used for holding lamp oil. The old monk said to him, "Tell me, son, about these two bottles."

The novice answered, "The bottle that has not held any oil is only dusty and dry. But the bottle that has been filled and unfilled of oil many times is clean and coated with fragrance."

"In the same way," said the old man, "you benefit from asking and doing and pondering these spiritual things, even if they later pass from your mind. They will change and fragrance you."

Stations of the Cross

"Oh dear, it's very difficult being a Catholic."

"Does it make much difference to you?"

"Of course. All the time."

"Well, I can't say I've noticed it. Are you struggling against temptation? You don't seem much more virtuous than me."

"I'm very, very much wickeder."

—Evelyn Waugh, *Brideshead Revisited*[12]

One of the most tenacious of Catholic devotions, the Stations of the Cross are usually represented as a series of fourteen pictures or sculptures hanging at eye level that represent the scenes of Jesus' final hours, from his condemnation by Pilate to the placing of his body in the tomb. Walking them in a church or outdoors or (God, please, one day) in Jerusalem on the path that Jesus himself walked, the Stations are our physical way of following Christ to Calvary. Doing them online will never quite replicate the same experience, although you'll find several places to do them there too.

Recognizing the Stations is an ancient devotion that was first organized into a spiritual practice in the fourteenth century by the Franciscans who became official custodians of the holy sites in the Holy Land. In the spirit of Saint Francis, the Stations are a way to—sometimes literally and certainly spiritually—follow in the steps of Christ. "Take up your cross and follow me," Jesus said to his disciples. That's precisely what the original Stations on the streets of Jerusalem purport to do. The first station, for example, begins in the courtyard of what is today, el-Omariye College, where Pilate's Praetorium and the Roman garrison once stood. It is there that Jesus was condemned to death by Pilate. At the site of other stations, the Franciscans have built chapels and memorials. Station Five, for instance, remembers when and where Simon of Cyrene carried the cross for Jesus; the physical spot is at the beginning of Market Road, which leads into Jerusalem. A small Franciscan chapel sits on this spot today. Stations Ten through Fourteen are actually located inside the Church of the Holy Sepulcher. The great church now occupies the space that once included Golgotha (another name for Calvary) as well as the tomb where Jesus was buried.

The traditional ordering of the fourteen scenes follows what scripture and tradition combine to say happened to Jesus on the way to Calvary (an asterisk indicates tradition rather than a biblical source for that stage):

1. Jesus is condemned to death.
2. Jesus receives the cross.
3. Jesus falls for the first time.*
4. Jesus sees his mother.*
5. Simon of Cyrene helps carry the cross.
6. Veronica wipes Jesus' face with her veil.*
7. Jesus falls for the second time.*
8. Jesus meets the women of Jerusalem.
9. Jesus falls for the third time.*

10. Jesus is stripped of his garments.
11. Jesus is nailed to the cross.
12. Jesus dies.
13. Jesus' body is removed from the cross.* (Imagined in Michelangelo's *Pietà I*)
14. Jesus is laid in the tomb.

Walking, remembering, and praying at each station is an exercise in humility and a corrective for reorienting the body and spirit to the true meaning of life. The Stations can be almost ubiquitous in Catholic churches, but that doesn't mean they are to be observed glibly. Part of doing them correctly is feeling the events deeply. Sorrow is a Catholic emotion, and replicating Christ's sorrow and that of his mother, Mary, is part of walking the Stations well. An African American spiritual understood the importance of following the Stations: "Were you there when they crucified my Lord? Oh, sometimes it causes me to tremble, tremble, tremble."

Most of us walk them in places other than Jerusalem. Find yourself a crucifix—preferably made of wood—or a rosary with a wooden crucifix, and walk them. Go to a church or space the fourteen Stations in your own backyard. Some of the great cathedrals in the world, such as Saint Patrick's in New York City or Santa Croce in Florence or Westminster Cathedral in London, offer the fourteen Stations spaced throughout their naves. Other churches have created indigenous versions, showing how the Way of Jesus is for all people. In Lodwar Cathedral in Kenya, for instance, the Stations were recently painted to reflect an African setting. The faces, clothing, and places are authentically Kenyan. Pilate is portrayed as a local chief in traditional African dress rather than as a Roman. Even the cross of Christ looks different—like the branch of an African tree.

I walk the Stations in snowshoes on the hillside behind my house in Vermont, most often at dusk. The advent of long nights is, for me, spiritually nourishing. Old logging trails and stone walls have become for me paths and chapels. The Stations are ideally represented pictorially, but I don't have that in my woods, and so I carry a devotional book with images of each of the fourteen. I walk them with book in hand.

Here is my closing prayer:

> Jesus, your life, passion, and death unite earth and heaven. Your sorrow accomplishes more than I will ever understand.
>
> Change in me all that needs converting, and give me the strength to follow in your steps.
>
> You, Grace, live and reign with the Father and the Holy Spirit one God, for ever and ever. Amen.

You may prefer to observe stations that are explicitly biblical in origin. Six of the original fourteen owe their origin to legend rather than the Gospel accounts. In response to such requests, Pope John Paul II praised the following reordering of the Stations, celebrating them for the first time in 1991. Each is derived directly from the Gospels:

1. Jesus agonizes in the Garden of Gethsemane (Matthew 25:36–41).
2. Jesus is betrayed by Judas and arrested (Mark 14:43–46).
3. Jesus is condemned by the Sanhedrin (Luke 22:66–71).
4. Jesus is denied by Peter (Matthew 26:69–75).
5. Jesus is condemned to death by Pilate (Mark 15:1–5, 15).
6. Jesus is scourged and crowned with thorns (John 19:1–3).
7. Jesus bears his cross (John 19:6, 15–17).

8. Simon of Cyrene helps carry the cross (Mark 15:21).
9. Jesus meets the women of Jerusalem (Luke 23:27–31).
10. Jesus is crucified (Luke 23:33–34).
11. Jesus promises paradise to the good thief (Luke 23:39–43).
12. Jesus speaks to Mary and the disciple from the cross (John 19:25–27).
13. Jesus dies on the cross (Luke 23:44–46).
14. Jesus is laid in the tomb (Matthew 27:57–60).

Remembering and honoring Christ's death in its details is a way to learn as a child learns to walk—to travel in his footsteps and prepare for eternal life.

Bones and Bodies

> "If I had my life over again I should form the habit of nightly composing myself to thoughts of death. . . . Death, when it approaches, ought not to take one by surprise. It should be part of the full expectancy of life. Without an ever-present sense of death life is insipid."
>
> —MURIEL SPARK, *MEMENTO MORI*[13]

Remember your death" is the best translation of the Latin phrase *memento mori*. Visual artists have painted many *memento mori* images over the centuries. One famous triptych by Hans Memling is titled *Earthly Vanity and Divine Salvation* and hangs in a museum in Strasbourg, France. In the three-part picture, a beautiful woman stands in the center panel, naked and holding a mirror to see herself, with lovely homes and gardens behind her and a pet dog by her side. Lurking on the panels beside her are, on the left, a dead body, once buried and now decomposing, and on the right, a devil tormenting humans in hell. Triptychs have a way of telling a story that gets our attention. A text from the Apocrypha often accompanies these images: "In everything you do, remember your end, and you will never sin" (Ecclesiasticus 7:36).

In Muriel Spark's novel *Memento Mori,* the most intriguing character is the anonymous one who telephones the highborn to say, "Remember, you must die." This, of course, unnerves people—especially the eccentric, wealthy ones who inhabit Spark's novels. These assorted friends seek out the advice of retired police inspector, Henry Mortimer. Mortimer eerily but obviously advises the group—in the sentences I've just quoted from the novel—to do what the anonymous caller is telling them to do. This is not the advice that they were seeking. In the end, we learn that it may have been the angel of death itself making the calls. Hardly a prank.

The ancients didn't joke about death. There is a story from ancient Rome that servants would sometimes remind their masters of their immortality. One of the most important early Christian apologists, Tertullian, wrote of this practice of slaves reminding their masters of death in his book *Apologeticus.* Tertullian explains why he would never call the Roman Emperor a "god.""He who calls him a god denies that he is an emperor. Unless he be a man he is not an emperor. That he is a man, he is admonished even when triumphing in his most lofty chariot. He is reminded from behind: 'Look behind thee; remember that thou art a man.'"[14] This doesn't seem to mesh with our usual image of the subjugated slave who serves his master in constant fear of offending. It is as if the servant symbolizes the weakness and frailty of humankind; to "look behind thee" means to look at the servant and to realize that the ultimate end of all people is bodily death.

In the centuries that followed Tertullian, reminders of death became personified in the form of the *danse macabre* ("dance of death"): plays and paintings depicting dancing skeletons, reeking corpses in the otherwise pastoral scenes, and the sort of happy-one-second-and-deadly-the-next flashpoints so common to horror films today. There was much death to characterize in those centuries, from the Black Death of plagues to wars that resulted in grisly events that make today's conflicts seem surgically neat to famines and pestilences—death was truly everywhere. The Middle Ages had few hospitals and hospices. Only the severely and obviously ill, such as lepers and plague sufferers, were quarantined. Otherwise, death occurred at home.

Biblical stories of death filled the medieval imagination. One story comes from the Apocryphal book (found in most Catholic Bibles) of 2 Maccabees, chapter 7. The story of torture and murder of a mother and her seven sons at the hands of a Greek king centered around the new king's attempts to force an end to Jewish ritual. Mothers were killed for circumcising their sons. Boys were murdered for observing the Sabbath. And Jews everywhere were slaughtered in the most heinous ways imaginable for refusing to eat sacrificial meals in honor of the king.

The story of the mother and her seven sons particularly captured the imagination of our medieval ancestors. They didn't read the murders as a king killing his subjects but as the character of Death holding sway over a time and place, much as they believed that Death held sway over their own time and place. It was difficult to see God at various times in the first twelve to fifteen centuries after Christ.

Today we have come full circle. Our problem is the reverse: we are comfortable in countries that are wealthier than any in history, and we are physically healthy in ways that are equally unprecedented. What do we know of the *danse macabre?* It does not haunt us in the ways that it once haunted our ancestors. Death has become sanitized, controlled, explicable, even planned. We even have death insurance; our loved ones will be provided for after we are gone. And some of us have "final expenses" insurance so that our loved ones won't even have to clean up after us. Some companies call this "whole life" insurance, which is ironic, because being willing to experience death and live with death is actually the key to understanding life that we have mostly forgotten.

Consider how burial practices have evolved in only the past thirty or forty years. It used to be common to have not only a wake and a funeral but also a service of burial at the grave site. When was the last time that you were able to add a shovelful or a handful of dirt to the grave of a friend or loved one? We hardly ever get to see the coffin or pine box or ashes go into the ground anymore, let alone see them buried. Why is it that the funeral companies want to shoo us away from the actual burial? It's as if someone decided that we were supposed to be shielded from that sort of finality.

We need death. We need it like we need the joy of life. There is perhaps no greater possibility for Christian witness today and in the future than to recover the Catholic attitude toward death. To be bad at dying is to be bad at living, and Christians are best able to show this truth in their lives. What would it mean if we were able to honestly say with Saint Paul, "Life to me, of course, is Christ, but then death would be a positive gain" (Philippians 1:21)? Such words roll far more easily off the tongue than they make sense in the ways we live our lives. It is good to die, and we must actually learn to want it—or at the very least, not fear it or make Herculean efforts to avoid it. Nothing is more Catholic than to show that we believe in resurrection, new life. Jesus taught in John 12:24, "In all truth I tell you, unless a wheat grain falls into the earth and dies, it remains only a single grain; but if it dies it yields a rich harvest."

You can still see in Europe and New England, among other older places, burial grounds that are snug up against the side of churches so that Christians can remember the martyrs and other faithful. This practice in fact originated with Christians, in contrast to the Romans, who had a saying, "The city is for the living, not the dead"—and used to bury outside the city walls.

I recently joined a handful of other pilgrims for Evensong at Canterbury Cathedral in England. It was a Thursday, but it happened to be the feast day for remembering one of the martyred medieval saints of Canterbury, and so six of us stayed afterward for Holy Communion. Only six in one of the largest and most beautiful church buildings in the world! The simple service took place in a small chapel that connects to the place where Thomas Becket was murdered by the knights of King Henry II. We were remembering one fallen saint—Elphege was his name—in a chapel a few paces from where Becket was killed. Bodies and bones were on my mind.

I was shocked, as I sat, to see the ornamentation on the side altar next to me. Femurs, skulls, and even what looked like a jawbone adorned the sides of the ornate table. They looked to be carved centuries ago from ivory or stone. But I shouldn't have been surprised; bodies and bones adorn churches around the world, and it isn't meant to be spooky, only to be a reminder of what the church is built on—the hope of resurrection that defeats death.

Polycarp (d. 155) was the bishop of Smyrna, in today's Turkey, and the last disciple of John, one of the original twelve apostles. He lived during a time when it was criminal to be Christian. To be Christian was to be an atheist in the eyes of the state because it entailed a refusal to worship the Roman emperor. We have an intricate account of what happened to Polycarp, even as he stood fast in his faith to the point of being burned at the stake. The *Martyrdom of Polycarp* records how his followers regarded the bishop's physical remains: "We at last gathered up his bones, which are more precious to us than precious gems and finer than gold, and laid them to rest where it was proper to do so. There the Lord will permit us to come together in gladness and joy to celebrate the birthday of his martyrdom."

Saint Paul wrote in his letter to the congregation in Philippi, "Brothers, be united in imitating me. Keep your eyes fixed on those who act according to the example you have from me" (Philippians 3:17). That is precisely what the people of Smyrna, and beyond, were doing when they reverenced the bones of Polycarp. They were according honor to the physical house where such holiness had been. Paul himself was martyred in the 60s in Rome. To be Catholic means that we do not believe in death. We believe in resurrection. So we don't reverence the bodies of the faithful because we are somehow pagan—quite the opposite! Saint Augustine compared the bones of the martyrs to the "limbs" of the Holy Spirit in late antiquity, and all Christians have believed (until very recently) fervently in the vision of Saint Paul offered in 1 Thessalonians 4:16–18:

> At the signal given by the voice of the Archangel and the trumpet of God, the Lord himself will come down from heaven; those who have died in Christ will be the first to rise, and only after that shall we who remain alive be taken up in the clouds, together with them, to meet the Lord in the air. This is the way we shall be with the Lord for ever. With such thoughts as these, then, you should encourage one another.

Medieval manuscripts are chock full of illustrations showing the bones and bodies of the faithful climbing out of their caskets, the earth, even the bellies of animals and sea creatures, to ascend into the air and join the returning Christ in glory. Bones were revered because they signify links between heaven and earth, between God's incarnation and our exercising it in our lives. After human death, the body only lays dormant, waiting for a later time to rise again.

Of course, there were abundant excesses. Various examples abound. There are at least three different groups throughout Europe that claim to have the head of Saint John the Baptist. Is it in the ancient Umayyad Mosque in Damascus, as is claimed by Muslims around the world? Did the Knights Templar take possession of it during the Crusades and return it to Rome, where it may also be seen on public display? There is even a strong tradition that the beheaded relic was long ago carried by Crusaders back to England and secretly buried in Halifax, West Yorkshire. The name Halifax is believed to mean "holy face," and the image of Saint John's face adorns the town's medieval coat of arms. This is the stuff of popular novels.

I remember when I took my kids to Canterbury Cathedral for the first time. I was anxious to tell them the stories of Thomas Becket in the twelfth century. Thomas was a complicated figure; he was a mix of publicity hound and genuine saint, having gone from politician without much regard for religion to devout archbishop in the span of only a few years. But his independent spirit put him at odds with his king, and Thomas had to flee England for the Continent for fear of his life. After a few years away, he courageously returned, knowing that he would probably die. "Someone needs to rid me of my archbishop!" King Henry infamously said, and a group of ambitious knights hunted Thomas down in his own cathedral.

This is the part that I mistakenly told my kids when they were about nine and eleven years old: one of the knights reached out to strike Thomas in the head as he knelt in prayer, and the blade of that sword sliced a piece of skull, spreading brains and blood all over the floor. The people ran in as the knights rode out, and they quickly began to gather up the blood and brains as holy relics. Unless you are a grossed-out nine-year-old, you cannot stand or kneel there without feeling the special presence of God.

To become familiar with bones and bodies is an important aspect of Catholic spirituality, reminding us that we do not believe in death but in resurrection. Ancient and medieval saints often kept skulls around as reminders of the brevity of life. Saints Jerome and Francis of Assisi are most commonly shown in this way. As a teenager, I used to stand in front of the Spanish painter El Greco's famous painting of Saint Francis in the Art Institute of Chicago, which shows the saint in bowed consideration of a crucifix, skull, and prayer book. It didn't make much sense to me then, but it does now. As the ancient liturgy still repeated at Anglican burials says, "In the midst of life we are in death." Bones become not only a reminder of death (*memento mori*) but also a tool for meditation.

Something Good About Hell

Here at least
We shall be free; the Almighty hath not built
Here for his envy, will not drive us hence:
Here we may reign secure; and in my choice
To reign is worth ambition, though in Hell:
Better to reign in Hell than serve in Heaven.

—JOHN MILTON, *PARADISE LOST*[15]

Lucifer loved his new digs in hell, according to Milton. But he's probably the only one. I'm not going there, and neither are any of my friends. In fact, no one I know or have ever met is headed there. Or at least that's how I like to think about it. Is hell a literal place? I don't know for sure, and Catholics are divided on that question.

But I believe I have known people who are in a very real way in hell right now. How else do you explain the way that people seem to sometimes die on the inside? Both sin and circumstance—without consciousness of grace and forgiveness—lead to hardening of hearts and the darkening of souls. I have seen souls slowly die.

Hell is the English translation of *Sheol,* the Hebrew name for the place of the departed. Throughout most of human history, people have believed in some place at the center of the earth to which certain souls enter upon death. Hell has evolved in our imaginations since the later Middle Ages, when Dante brought it most vividly to life.

The *Catechism of Christian Doctrine,* a little instructional book that was popular in England and Ireland nearly two centuries ago (also called the *Penny Catechism* because it cost only a penny), posed Socratic-style questions and answers that raised millions of school-age children in the basic tenets of faith. If you were raised on it, you probably remember the first three entries with precision:

1. Who made you?
   God made me.
2. Why did God make you?
   God made me to know Him, love Him and serve Him in this world, and be happy with Him forever in the next.
3. To whose image and likeness did God make you?
   God made me to His own image and likeness.

Under "The Twelfth Article of the [Nicene] Creed," the *Penny Catechism* offers:

130. What is the twelfth article of the Creed?
   The twelfth article of the Creed is "life everlasting."
131. What does "life everlasting" mean?
   "Life everlasting" means that the good shall live forever in the glory and happiness of heaven.

132. What is the glory and happiness of heaven?
The glory and happiness of heaven is to see, love, and enjoy God forever.

133. What does the Scripture say of the happiness of heaven?
The Scripture says of the happiness of heaven: "That eye hath not seen, nor ear heard, neither hath it entered into the heart of man, what things God hath prepared for them that love him." (1 Cor. 2:9)

134. Shall not the wicked also live forever?
The wicked also shall live and be punished forever in the fire of hell.

It was not long ago when most Catholics believed that mortal sins such as deliberately missing Mass and telling a lie to one's parents could send one to hell if they went unconfessed before death. The existence of both heaven and hell was assumed by nearly all Christians—Catholic or not—before the twentieth century. But today hell has gone the way of the holy obligation and the unforgivable sin. They no longer exist for the majority of the faithful.

As a place, hell has faded away. It is no longer believed by most Christians to be a physical place where God punishes disbelief (even though we find it easier to believe in heaven). I certainly don't believe that hell is final and irrevocable, as the book of Revelation and medieval theologians once taught. And I don't accept the vengeful and voluptuous images in verse and paint of people like Dante and Hieronymus Bosch who seemed to delight in imagining people they knew being tormented in that fiery place.

In his book *Eschatology,* Cardinal Joseph Ratzinger (now Pope Benedict XVI) wrote a beautiful explanation of what Christ did when he descended into hell (as we proclaim in the Apostle's Creed) after his Crucifixion during the time known to tradition as Holy Saturday:

> God himself suffered and died. . . . He himself entered into the distinctive freedom of sinners, but he went beyond it in that freedom of his own love which descended willingly into the Abyss. . . . It is a challenge to suffer in the dark night of faith, to experience communion with Christ in solidarity with his descent into the Night. One draws near to the Lord's radiance by sharing his darkness.[16]

This would seem to suggest that we all belong in hell, if only for a time. Certainly we all experience pain, separation from God, loneliness, a feeling of futility, and loss of self. These are symptoms. But most people who experience these things do not hold on to them in such a way that hell becomes the only place where they feel comfortable. Most of us heal. We get better.

Many of us now chalk hell up as a sick medieval fantasy, a place where it was once convenient to posit your enemies. The great architect of that awful place, Dante, did just that. But in her terrific translation of Dante's *Divine Comedy,* Dorothy Sayers explains, "It is not a fairy-story, but a great Christian allegory, deriving its power from the terror and splendor of the Christian revelation."[17] Terror and splendor indeed. It is true. Jesus taught his followers to believe in hell in ways that were uncommon for Jewish teachers of his time.

Read the parable of the wedding feast in Matthew 22. Jesus tells the story of a king's wedding feast for his son as a way to understand the kingdom of heaven. The preparations for the feast completed, the king instructs his servants to gather all of the invited guests. No one appears. Not wanting to embarrass his son, the king asks his servants to go to the crossroads and invite everyone they see to come to the feast. Eventually, the hall is filled with guests, most of them, no doubt, confused even as to the name of the bride and groom. At that point in the parable, Jesus says, "When the king came in to see the guests, he noticed a man there who was not wearing a wedding garment, and he said to him, 'Friend, how did you get in here without a wedding robe?' And he was speechless. Then the king said to the attendants, 'Bind his hand and foot and throw him into the outer darkness, where there will be weeping and grinding of teeth.' For many are called, but few are chosen." When was the last time you heard someone preach a sermon on that passage?

The medievals were not far off when they decided that the Christ who sits in judgment is scary, while the Virgin Mary is the mother who always loves us and welcomes our entreaties. One of the most popular images of God in Dante's day was of Christ seated in heaven, holding the earth like a grapefruit in the palm of his hand. Medieval penitents pleaded with Mary, asking her to convince Jesus to show mercy and not squish them all.

A Catholic spirituality believes that each human being has a soul, a free will to choose, and that every day is full of opportunities to accept or reject God. In addition—and this is the kicker—only in death will we realize exactly how we have chosen. The historian Eamon Duffy explained in *Faith of Our Fathers:*

> We believe in hell, because we can imagine ourselves choosing it. We cannot know the secrets of other people's souls, but we know enough of our own to recognize something within us which shies away from God, something which wants to close our hearts to others. There is no inevitability about our response to God or to other people: hate and fear, as well as love and

> trust, are close to hand. Hell, in that sense, is a perpetual calling within us, from which only the loving mercy of God holds us back. . . . Hell remains a terrible possibility, the dark side of our freedom. But the last word in all this belongs not with our freedom, but with God's grace.[18]

That's just it: "We believe in hell, because we can imagine ourselves choosing it. . . . But the last word in all this belongs not with our freedom, but with God's grace." That's what I call something good about hell. Hell reminds us of who we could be, without Christ. And God reminds us of his grace in Christ, which is for us in spite of our freedom.

I believe what I pray. At each Baptism in the Episcopal Church, the congregation prays:

LEADER: Deliver them, O Lord, from the way of sin and death.

PEOPLE: Lord, hear our prayer.

In the Nicene Creed, we say that we believe in "life everlasting." At the graveside, as we commit a dead friend or loved one to the ground, I believe it when I pray:

> In the midst of life we are in death. . . .
> Thou knowest, Lord, the secrets of our hearts;
> shut not thy merciful ears to our prayer;
> but spare us, Lord most holy, O God most mighty,
> O holy and merciful Savior,
> thou most worthy Judge eternal.
> Suffer us not, at our last hour,
> through any pains of death, to fall from thee.

Meister Eckhart once said that he would love Jesus Christ even if he was condemned to hell. That seems to capture the essence of the Catholic spirit. And Eckhart came from an era that believed in the existence of hell as a place of torment, unreservedly!

Heaven and hell are not geographic places so much as they are states of being. It is for this reason that each state begins during our earthly lives: we either grow to know our true selves, ending our lives with a measure of joy and love that deepens into God, or we lose sight of what is true and instead fashion a false self that leads into alienation, darkness, and pain beyond death.

Evil is not necessarily bad; sometimes it is exactly what we need to see clearly what is good—for us and for God. This is what Saint Augustine meant when he exclaimed "*Felix culpa*!" ("O happy fault!"). On a more sober note, the poet John Donne wrote, memorably, wishing for punishment in the form of penitence:

> O Saviour, as thou hang'st upon the tree;
> I turn my back to thee, but to receive
> Corrections, till thy mercies bid thee leave.
> O think me worth thine anger, punish me,
> Burn off my rusts, and my deformity,
> Restore thine Image, so much, by thy grace,
> That thou may'st know me, and I'll turn my face.[19]

Nevertheless, we rest in the promise of the disciple whom Jesus loved: "My little children, I am writing this to you so that you do not sin; but if any one does sin, we have an Advocate with the Father, Jesus Christ the Just One. He is the expiation for our sins, and not for our sins only, but also for the sins of the whole world" (John 2:1–2).

SECTION FOUR

MUCH MORE THAN KITSCH AND JESUS JUNK

Rosary Beads

> In order to say the rosary, one does not need to know much if anything about the history of the practice. It was for a long time shrouded in legend.
>
> —Gary Wills, *The Rosary*[1]

The same practices that draw me to Catholic spirituality are often the ones that repel those who were raised Catholic. The Irish novelist John McGahern displayed what must be called a love-hate relationship with his childhood Catholicism in early novels like *The Dark* and *The Barracks.* The stuff he pokes fun at is precisely what I have been incorporating furiously into my life. Nighttime prayers, rosaries, blessings, ritual, devotions, and pieties became something inflexible, overbearing, and oppressive in his rural Catholic upbringing. Religion can so completely consume a life that it becomes something to fight. I certainly went through similar experiences with my evangelical Protestantism in my teens and early twenties. In fact, I better understand another novelist, D. H. Lawrence, reflecting on his own Protestant upbringing:

> From earliest years . . . I had the Bible poured every day into my helpless consciousness, till there came almost a saturation point. . . . This Bible language . . . affected all the processes of emotion and thought. So that today, although I have *forgotten* my Bible, I need only begin to read a chapter to realize that I *know* it with an almost nauseating fixity.[2]

These interior battles are the essence of any genuine and real response to God.

The pieties of faith—those ancient practices that quietly bind us to each other and to those who have come before us—are also the first to go in times of doubt or trouble. Even if you learned from your grandmother how and why to pray your rosary, you may stop fingering your beads when a local priest disappoints you. Even though I know that dropping to my knees links me to the earliest Christians who honored the name of Jesus, it will begin to feel like nonsense to me to kneel, rise, and kneel again when people in my church are bickering.

Lawrence Cunningham, a theology professor at the University of Notre Dame, recently explained:

> Within the broad Catholic tradition . . . spirituality has meant, and continues to mean, the ways in which people, beyond the ordinary practices of the faith, have sought to live their Christian lives more intensely. . . . By "more intensely" I mean the sort of religious attention that goes beyond the ordinary observances of practicing Catholics in the sacramental life of the church.[3]

This is what is best about being Catholic.

If evangelical Protestants have what I might playfully call "Jesus junk" (Jesus rag dolls, little mints with Bible verses on them, and so on), Roman Catholics have kitsch—commercially produced items that are designed to appeal to popular tastes and often considered lowbrow or tacky). I actually appreciate it all, to a point, but occasionally it begins to reek of consumerism run amok. Just the other day, I received the mail order catalogue of one of the largest companies dealing in Catholic kitsch. It was the "Easter/Confirmation Season" issue. Scanning its hundred pages of products, I saw that I could purchase Saints Trading Cards (jumbo pack of 100, $29.95), First Communion Hankies (12 inches by 12 inches, cotton, $5.95), Holy Water from Lourdes (1 oz. with prayer card, $3.00), and a statue of Pope John Paul II (resin on wood base with removable crosier, $65.00). Funny thing is, I'd enjoy having them all. Well, not the hankies.

What is junk or kitsch to some is spiritual practice to others. And all of this stuff is for the purpose of learning how to practice and embody spirituality. There is a story about one of the Desert Fathers, Abba Cronius, that illustrates this point. One of the disciples of Cronius was a young man named Isaac, who came to stay with the revered Abba ("father"), wanting to learn all that the great man could teach him about life and faith. Isaac later reported, "He would never tell me what to do, even though he was old and frail and at least needed assistance with daily chores. But he would not tell me anything. The Abba did all himself, preparing food, serving it, setting the table for us and our guests. Finally, I asked the old man, 'Why don't you ask me to help, or tell me what to do?' He did not reply." And so Isaac left their dwelling to find other revered abbas in order to ask them what he was doing wrong. These colleagues of Abba Cronius accompanied the boy back to Cronius to speak on the boy's behalf. They said, "Abba, this young brother has come to learn from you and to help you. Why don't you tell him anything?" Abba Cronius looked at the group of men and then the boy and said, "Am I a ruler, that I should be ordering people around? If you wish to learn, do as I do." At that, Isaac understood, and he went on to learn plenty, becoming one of the Desert Fathers himself.

My first strand of beads was put into my hands by a friend who knew that I needed it. A Methodist, of all people, saw that I was lonely and looking for entertainment more often than being quiet and contemplative. "Have you ever tried one of these?" she said, with the innocence of someone who had recently picked one up herself.

The rosary beads she gave me were handmade by nuns in the American Southwest. I sometimes wish that I had a rosary that my grandparents had passed on to me, but they gave up their Irish and Italian Catholicism after they arrived in this country over a century ago. Anyway, this particular rosary was my first, and you always love your first. The San Damiano crucifix of Francis of Assisi hangs at the end, representing the icon that Francis knelt before in the abandoned church of San Damiano when he heard God speak to him for the first time.

I carry the prayer beads with me every day in my pocket along with wallet, business cards, and Palm Pilot. I don't carry them as a talisman to ward off evil or as a good luck charm. But I do keep them in my pocket precisely so that I will be reminded of them, of my prayers, and of Christ throughout the day.

The *Catechism* wisely states, "In the living tradition of prayer, each Church proposes to its faithful, according to its historic, social, and cultural context, a language for prayer: words, melodies, gestures, iconography" (para. 2663). *Words. Melodies. Gestures. Iconography.* A world of divine good in those four words.

But it is also OK to make up your own words to go with the beads on your rosary, selecting from the many traditions that abound for praying with them. Plenty of pamphlets will tell you the words to use and how to make your way around the strand; there are Web sites, too; and of course, any priest would be happy to show you how. The most important thing is to pray it and to allow your prayers to be repetitious. The Protestant mind rebels against repetition in spirituality, whereas the Catholic imagination understands that repetition schools the heart.

Little Books

> You ought to sometimes be in your room, in your garden, or elsewhere, where you may be better able, according to your own desire, to withdraw your spirit within your heart and refresh your soul with good meditation and holy thoughts, or a little good reading.
>
> —Saint Francis de Sales, *The Devout Life*

The two books dearest to me are my grandfather's old Scofield King James Bible and my nineteenth-century Book of Common Prayer. The Scofield is thick and weighty with opinion and commentary. My grandpa used to shake it from behind the pulpit while he preached his long sermons in Baptist churches. The prayer book, meanwhile, is miniature (about 2¼ inches wide and 3¼ inches tall), and when my eyes go the way of Saint Lucy, I'll never be able to read its print. But at least for now, my little prayer book is complete with Psalter laid out according to the old method of reading it through completely on mornings and evenings each month. In contrast to what publishers today call books for the pocket, this one actually fits there.

The big black Scofield is the only thing I inherited from my grandfather. I'm glad to have it, and I read it from time to time, whenever I want to be reminded of the poetry of the King James. But its size is not an accident. The Scofield was the most Protestant of Bibles, with notes and glosses galore; it had a lot to say. Today I prefer more Catholic books, and it is no accident that many of them are little.

Saint Teresa of Avila once said that she frequently carried a small book with her into prayer, even if she might never open it, as a holy companion and support. I have always been drawn to little books. When I am in used bookstores, I pause to look at almost every small volume. It could be a photograph collection of the nineteenth-century railroads of western North Carolina, but if it is small in format and cozy-feeling in the palm, I'm interested. Just the other day, I purchased three books from the dealer nearest my home in Vermont—small editions of Thomas Merton's *Seeds of Contemplation* and two of those terrific, old, early New Directions "paperbooks" of Denise Levertov poems with sewn bindings.

Little did I know, years ago, that loving little books was preparing me to appreciate Catholic piety. These are all objects used for the many pieties that fall under Catholic tradition: prayer collections, saints' lives, novenas (devotions consisting of prayers said, most typically, on nine successive days, asking to obtain special graces), books of blessings, and catechisms (penny catechisms!). All of these are found in little books. The seventeenth-century poet Richard Crashaw once wrote 118 lines on the power of a little prayer book in his life, these included:

You'll find it yields
To holy hands, and humble hearts,

> More swords and shields
> Than sin has snares, or hell has darts.[4]

Their often-gilded pages repel the clever people who disparage the things that I enjoy. God, give me pieties, rather than cleverness! As an evangelical child, I, too, mocked the simplemindedness of bowing, kneeling, fingering beads, and praying the same thing over and over again, but now I want these things in order to save my life from the monotony of spontaneity. When I was more Protestant, I believed that piety needed defending—as if it were something to apologize for having or doing—but now I wish for the authenticity possible within its practices. Little books are chief among the *things* that carry spiritual meaning in my life.

Little books can go anywhere. They were once the most incendiary and dangerous way to affect opinion and change, as when Martin Luther was picking fights with cardinals and popes in the early sixteenth century, quickly writing and publishing his little tracts to fire the bellies of Germans and Christians everywhere. Actually, the Reformation was fueled by little books. For the decade or so when his life was in constant danger, Luther was always waiting anxiously for some small tract to get off the press. He believed that each one would sway public opinion to his causes, and they often did. The Dutch humanist and theologian Erasmus also used little books—intended to entertain, using sarcasm, puns, proverbs, and other forms of witticism—to fuel the Renaissance. Erasmus wrote a series of what were called "colloquies," entertaining short plays used to teach and learn Latin, and he compiled many volumes of short proverbs from literature around the world. People laughed at Erasmus' little books, and he was glad. Luther once compared Erasmus to a slippery eel that only God could catch.

If you ask a Catholic mother or grandmother to turn her pockets inside out, you may find a rosary, but look on her night table, and you'll probably find some little books. Fewer people read books today than a decade ago, but the truth is that there have never been a lot of book readers. Most people don't see books as useful. People in all eras have placed more importance on good food and drink and other forms of entertainment than on words, which have been regarded as mostly harmless but of marginal value to daily life.

The book as we know it has been around for about eighteen hundred years. The papyrus rolls of Socrates and Julius Caesar were replaced with the more portable, compact, and easily navigated codex. The codex, the book's ancestor before the printing press, probably originated in the second century.

Christians championed the codex over the roll from the beginning. There are no extant copies of the New Testament, for instance, written on rolls; the early ones are all codices. Perhaps this was because in the beginning, Christianity was an alien faith. It was easier to read a codex in private or in smaller ways than a roll. When parchment (made of sheepskin) replaced papyrus (reeds) as the pages of codices, this also added to their portability. (It also required the slaughter of many animals. Early manuscripts of the entire Bible often required the skins of as many as five hundred sheep.) But the average codex was smaller and lighter than earlier rolls, making possible the poetry of faith and the treasury of expression. If the roll was designed for public reading, the codex and book were meant for the savoring of words. And the ability of the codex to combine an anthology of writings suited the publishing of the scriptures just right.

After the collapse of the Roman Empire in the fifth century, the world of learning teetered on the edge of extinction. Monks and monasteries stepped in and became the only safe places for the copying, preservation, and distribution of books.

For this reason, most of the earliest surviving books are religious ones. What else would be precious enough to copy by hand onto expensive handmade paper and vellum? There are religious books from the Middle Ages that weigh five to ten pounds with wooden bindings; these were usually housed in monastery scriptoriums and moved about like ancient relatives, on trolleys.

Just as the spiritual practice of *lectio divina,* listening for God's voice while reading, was nurtured in monasteries, the preparation of books was a holy process, as much a prayer as those that were said in church. Recipes were created for different inks, which often included instructions such as "Begin to boil the gall nuts in vinegar. Say two Paternosters and three Ave Marias. Drain." Everything about books began and ended with faith. Even with the advent of the first printing presses, it was Bibles and religious tracts that kept them busy in the late 1400s.

Monks also produced books of prayer for individuals outside the monasteries, such as the popular Book of Hours, which were volumes of special prayers used to mark each day with spiritual meaning. These were usually commissioned by wealthy patrons and hand-copied by scribes. Artists decorated the edges of the pages, even on the smallest of surfaces, and sometimes put an image of the owner of the book into one of the opening illustrations, in a gesture of prayer. These books became objects and actions of faith, not just boards that held together descriptions of faith.

From these beginnings come the little devotional books of Catholic tradition. The small-format paperback novel of entertainment that one buys today at the grocery store is a modern invention, but small books have always been among the faithful. Throughout the Middle Ages, they seem to have gotten smaller and smaller. The average pocket of a pilgrim in Geoffrey Chaucer's day was far more generous than a blue jeans pocket today. But the size of little books has for the most part remained a constant four by seven inches, give or take. There are even tinier books that fit in the palm of an adult hand, such as my little prayer book. It is this handheld devotion that I like most of all. Novenas. Little Offices (official prayers whereby the hours of the day are consecrated to God). Tracts of the Seven Penitential Psalms (Psalms 6, 32, 38, 51, 102, 130, and 143). The Book of Hours (a collection of texts, prayers, and psalms, along with appropriate illustrations, to form a reference for worship and devotion).

There have been many times in history when little books changed the world. Small booklets of prayers to the Virgin and reflections on the Magnificat of Mary were distributed among César Chávez's farmworkers in the 1960s in California and among Guatemalans in the 1980s.

The prophet Jeremiah said to God, "Thy words were found, and I did eat them" (Jeremiah 15:16). Words have always mattered to Christians. We are "people of the Word," and words of prayer and praise have power to actually make happen what they entreat and proclaim. That is why we love to write in our books, and I love to buy secondhand books that are full of someone else's marginalia, underlinings, exclamation points, and question marks. I treasure a little book of the mystical teachings of Saint John of the Cross that was originally published and purchased in the 1950s by a woman whom I have never met but who apparently lived in the town next to mine. I bought her book for a buck from the "Really Cheap" carton sitting outside my local shop. She wrote her name, city and state, and "Advent 1954" on the front pastedown. Margaret G. may actually be dead by now, but I have learned much from her thoughtful notes, scribbled all over the margins. Margaret G. starred and bracketed things, underlining meaningful passages, pointing me to what John of the Cross has to say for my life too.

Images That Speak

> "My father, faced with an unfamiliar notion, is like a cow staring at a new barn door. Like those who look on the cross and see nothing. All they hear is the priest's forgiveness."
>
> —JOHN OSBORNE, *LUTHER*[5]

Looking deeper into the meaning of things—that is what Catholics try to learn to do. My more Protestant imagination often has little room for anything but words. Scripture reading, preaching, the finer points of what is and is not to be believed by the head—that was once the exclusive stuff of my spirituality. In fact, it wasn't stuff at all. It was antistuff.

The attitude toward icons in my childhood faith was like that of historical iconoclasts (literally, those who deliberately destroy a culture's religious icons and other symbols or monuments, usually for religious or political motives). But in truth, religion of the head can become an idol as well and can make an idol of God. In these lines from Psalm 115, denouncing idolatry, notice still the emphasis on speaking, seeing, hearing, smelling, and touching:

> Their idols are silver and gold, the work of human hands.
>
> They have mouths, but they cannot speak; eyes have they, but they cannot see;
>
> They have ears, but they cannot hear; noses, but they cannot smell;
>
> They have hands, but they cannot feel; feet, but they cannot walk; they make no sound with their throat.
>
> Those who make them are like them, and so are all who put their trust in them.

A spiritual life is inextricable from the senses because we follow an incarnate God.

During a week in Advent in 1643, William Dowsing wrote in his diary about three venerable places in Cambridge, England, where he would destroy religious images for the glory of God: Peterhouse, King's College, and Saint Mary the Great. Dowsing was a Puritan iconoclast, and he considered that title a badge of honor, given to him by the earl of Manchester.

In Suffolk a month later, Dowsing would record in his diary, "We brake down about a hundred superstitious pictures; and seven fryers hugging a nun; and the picture of God, and Christ; and divers others very superstitious . . . and we beat down a great stoneing cross on the top of the church."[6] It was during the Oliver Cromwell era in England that a Puritan parliament ruled and attempted to remove anything left that was "papal," "Roman," or Catholic. Their intentions were of the highest order. They believed that religious images were forbidden by the injunction in the Old Testament book of Leviticus against making idols. By destroying the faces of angels and saints with their chisels, they thought they were refocusing the faithful on God alone.

A lack of imagination plagues the majority of human beings—just as the character of Martin Luther complains about his father in John Osborne's play. Unable to see beyond the physical, and listening to voices that have declared belief to be about things unseen, many decide to forgo the visual reminders and passages of faith that were treasured by our ancestors.

The English word *icon* comes from a Greek word that means "portrait." But an icon is not a portrait in the way we commonly think of one. Strictly speaking, there wasn't any art in the medieval imagination; what we appreciate today as fine art was for the medieval person devotional objects—icons, illuminated manuscripts, pectoral crosses. These things hang in museums today, but they were never intended for that purpose.

The *Catechism of the Catholic Church* explains how sacred images work in a spiritual life:

> The icon cannot represent the invisible and incomprehensible God, but the incarnation of the Son of God has ushered in a new "economy" of images: "Previously God, who has neither a body nor a face, absolutely could not be represented by an image. But now that he has made himself visible in the flesh and has lived with men, I can make an image of what I have seen of God . . . and contemplate the glory of the Lord, his face unveiled."
>
> Christian iconography expresses in images the same Gospel message that Scripture communicates by words. Image and word illuminate each other: "We declare that we preserve intact all the written and unwritten traditions of the Church which have been entrusted to us. One of these traditions consists in the production of representational artwork, which accords with the history of the preaching of the Gospel. For it confirms that the

> incarnation of the Word of God was real and not imaginary, and to our benefit as well, for realities that illustrate each other undoubtedly reflect each other's meaning" [paras. 1159–1160].

Icons are painted and they are sculpted; they are enormous and they are portable; they are intended to hang in churches and they are handheld. They are objects and they are sacred images. Above all, they not only represent the figure whom they portrait but also represent the person's actual presence. Icons of Christ are by far the most popular and most important of all. Praying with an icon is to look upon the icon of Christ as if it is Christ himself. Pray before the real and present Jesus, as represented in the image.

A Catholic imagination can sometimes hear an image speak. Francis of Assisi heard an icon of Christ (the San Damiano icon) tell him, "Go and rebuild my church, because as you can see, it is falling down." He took it quite literally and began gathering stones.

Francis was spending lots of quiet time by himself in those days, wandering around the town of Assisi and outside of it, into the countryside and craggy spots on the side of Mount Subasio. Being alone was not natural for Francis. He most likely hated it at the beginning. With the spirit of a poet and a romantic, he had always experienced himself in the context of others. Francis was the teenager who was always at the center of the party, wooing girls from their windows late at night, being chided by neighbors and friends who nevertheless admired his ardor and love for life. But circumstances led Francis to turn away from these things. He came to realize that these were aspects of his false self, and he had to spend time alone and in quiet in order to find his true self.

Francis began to wander. As always happens, physical movement led to spiritual movement. Walking for hours forced his spirit to kindle, and he began to see things in his life with the help of God in ways that were probably not possible before. Kneeling in old churches caused his heart to bow as well, and he sorrowed for his sins as he saw Christ's sorrow in a way that he hadn't seen it previously in church. Talking as if to himself but really to the creatures that he came upon, Francis learned to connect with creation in the way of the prophet who could see a future where "mountains and hills will break into joyful cries before you and all the trees of the countryside clap their hands" (Isaiah 55:12).

Catholics—and saints in general—do these things. Joan of Arc heard voices and was eventually burned at the stake for it. The descendants of her tormentors later apologized and made her a saint.

An icon is an image that acts as a doorway to God. It is extremely personal. The iconographer paints the eyes of the figures last because they are the most important aspect. The eyes of an image icon can speak to you. One of the most famous icons in the world is *Our Lady of Czestochowa* in Poland. To this day, it is a major destination of pilgrimage, and thousands of Poles and others have claimed to be healed in various ways as a result of asking her to intercede on their behalf. Our Lady of Czestochowa is a dark Madonna. One fifteenth-century writer said that this remarkable, dark image has "a gentle aspect whichever way you turn, which is said to have been one taken from among those which St. Luke the Evangelist painted with his own hand . . . and if you filled it with singular devotion, you would see it looking at you as if alive."[7]

The chronicler makes an interesting connection: between devotion and sight. Praying with icons uses the senses to come closer to the divine. As Jim Forest once said, "God is not an idea and praying is not an exercise to improve our idea of God, though for those of us who have spent a good deal of our lives in classrooms, it can be difficult to get beyond the world of ideas. Prayer is the cultivation of the awareness of God's actual presence."[8]

Novenas for Heathens and Outcasts

"Father, haven't you any comfort to give me? He was a bad Catholic."

"That's the silliest phrase in common use," Father Rank said.

"The Church says . . ."

"I know the Church says. The Church knows all the rules. But it doesn't know what goes on in a single human heart."

—GRAHAM GREENE, *THE HEART OF THE MATTER*[9]

I hate committee meetings and bureaucratic mumbo-jumbo. The organized Church is full of it. But I was recently appointed to a committee that sits at the heart of one of the most bureaucratic activities of Church business. It is called a "discernment committee," and we are primarily responsible for judging who is fit and not fit for priestly ministry in our diocese.

George Bernard Shaw once said, "The Churches must learn humility as well as teach it. The Apostolic Succession cannot be secured or confined by the laying on of hands: the tongues of fire have descended on heathens and outcasts too often for that, leaving anointed Churchmen to scandalize History as worldly rascals."[10] Even those of us who are so much on the inside of Church activity that we decide who should be ordained and who should not must remember how often the rebel, the heathen, and the outcast have emerged to bring light to religious darkness.

Shaw was writing about Joan of Arc, the teenage girl who heard voices—those of Saint Michael the Archangel's and Saint Catherine—telling her to fight the British for the sake of her French homeland. Joan's story is legendary. Born around 1412, she was a girl soldier who took the unprecedented step of boldly leading French troops at Orleans and repelling the British toward the end of the Hundred Years' War. Largely because of Joan, the French king, Charles VII, was coronated at Reims—an event that pleased Joan immensely. But only two years later, when she was just nineteen, Joan was charged with heresy and burned at the stake by British priests of the Roman Catholic Church in the Anglo-Norman city of Rouen (part of modern-day France). The year was 1431.

Joan's piety during her trial became legendary. All of her responses to the politically motivated questions and entrapments that led to her conviction were recorded for posterity. "Jesus" was the last word on her lips as the flames rose up the scaffold and enveloped her tiny body. Her ashes were scattered into the River Seine, and within days, talk of her saintliness began to spread from those who witnessed her trial and even among those who had unfairly interrogated her. Three of her accusers, including the bishop, Pierre Cauchon, died of various diseases within weeks. Within twenty-four years of her martyrdom, the case was reopened by the pope, and the conviction was overturned. Some four hundred years later, she was canonized by the Church that killed her.

The preface to Shaw's powerful play, *Saint Joan,* is as interesting as the drama itself. It combines Shaw's trademark wit and sarcasm with his also frequent theological insight. Shaw is the quintessential agnostic who possessed more faith than most of the faithful. In the first paragraph, Shaw refers to Joan as "the queerest fish among the eccentric worthies of the Middle Ages" and "one of the first Protestant martyrs." That last phrase has always rankled Catholics, particularly since Joan's canonization in 1920; but Shaw's point is that in her free-spirited defense of individual conscience over Church, she was indeed perhaps the first Protestant martyr.

In fact, there is always room—or at least there had better be—in the Church for the rebel, heathen, or outcast. Joan was none of these, but she *was* what we might call a fugitive. Just as there are many in the Church who follow the rules and obey the commandments and listen to those in authority, there must also be room for the prophetic ones among us who appear to be wrong, misguided, headstrong, and foolish but turn out years later to have been right all along. These are the fugitives. God knows we need them!

In the epilogue to *Saint Joan,* one of Joan's priestly accusers, Cauchon, encounters another priest after her death who says that he was redeemed and saved when he saw Joan die. Cauchon argues with this other priest—his name in the play is De Stogumber—saying that the suffering and example of Christ should be enough and that in essence, reformers are unnecessary. Cauchon responds, "Must then a Christ perish in torment in every age to save those that have no imagination?"

In my work on the discernment committee, I have decided that I must be on the lookout for that outlaw like Joan: the person who does not seem buttoned-up enough to lead by the standard guidelines but who we need to lead nonetheless. These people are often the ones we perceive as the rebels and heathens in our midst. They may refer to themselves as "lapsed" Catholics or former Christians, no longer interested in what the Church has to say. They are often the most sincere of spiritual people, seeking truth and not finding it in many places, both in the churches and out. They are unlike the closest disciples of Jesus, who, after all, were the only ones closest to Our Lord to betray him, deny him, and fall asleep on him, most fully in his time of need.

I pray the following novena—a series of related prayers repeated with concentrated attention for nine days—for all rebels, fugitives, and reformers who challenge those of us in the churches. Novenas have been used for millennia to prepare Catholics for special moments and to remember certain events before God. *Novenas* (derived from the Latin word for "nine") are prayed in the spirit of the disciples of Jesus who were holed up for nine days between the Ascension and the Day of Pentecost. Setting aside nine days for repeating the same petition or remembering the same loved one immediately after his or her death or preparing for an important feast can bring the person who prays into unity with Divine will and affection in ways that are unavailable by other means.

A NOVENA FOR REBELS AND HEATHENS IN THE CHURCH

(Note: If you are praying with others, appoint a leader who will pray the primary parts. *Group responses are in italics.*)

In the name of the Father, the Son, and the Holy Spirit.
Amen.

As the psalmist says,

I hear a voice I had not known. (Psalm 81:5)[11]

And

I will listen to what the Lord is saying, for he is speaking peace to his faithful people and to those who turn their hearts to him. (Psalm 85:8)

As we well know,

The Lord has not dealt with us according to our sins, nor rewarded us according to our wickedness. (Psalm 103:10)

A Reading from the Torah: Exodus 3:1–11
Moses was keeping the flock of his father-in-law Jethro, the priest of Midian; he led his flock beyond the wilderness, and came to Horeb, the mountain of God. There the angel of the LORD appeared to him in a flame of fire out of a bush; he looked, and the bush was blazing, yet it was not consumed. Then Moses said, "I must turn aside and look at this great sight, and see why the bush is not burned up." When the Lord saw that he had turned aside to see, God called to him out of the bush, "Moses, Moses!" And he said, "Here I am." Then he said, "Come no closer! Remove the sandals from your feet, for the place on which you are standing is holy ground." He said further, "I am the God of your father, the God of Abraham, the God of Isaac, and the God of Jacob." And Moses hid his face, for he was afraid to look at God.

Then the Lord said, "I have observed the misery of my people who are in Egypt; I have heard their cry on account of their taskmasters. Indeed, I know their sufferings, and I have come down to deliver them from the Egyptians, and to bring them up out of that land to a good and broad land, a land flowing with milk and honey, to the country of the Canaanites, the Hittites, the Amorites, the Perizzites, the Hivites, and the Jebusites. The cry of the Israelites has now come to me; I have also seen how the Egyptians oppress them. So come, I will send you to Pharaoh to bring my people, the Israelites, out of Egypt." But Moses said to God, "Who am I that I should go?" (NRSV)

Response

Blessed are the poor in spirit.

The kingdom of heaven is theirs.

Blessed are the pure in heart.

They shall see God.

Psalm 113

Give praise, you servants of the LORD; praise the Name of the LORD.

Let the Name of the LORD be blessed, from this time forth for evermore.

From the rising of the sun to its going down let the Name of the LORD be praised.

The LORD is high above all nations, and his glory above the heavens.

Who is like the LORD our God, who sits enthroned on high but stoops to behold the heavens and the earth?

He takes up the weak out of the dust and lifts up the poor from the ashes.

He sets them with the princes, with the princes of his people.

He makes the woman of a childless house to be a joyful mother of children.

A Reading from the Gospel: Matthew 26:36–40

Then Jesus came with them to a plot of land called Gethsemane; and he said to his disciples, "Stay here while I go over there to pray." He took Peter and the two sons of Zebedee with him. And he began to feel sadness and anguish.

Then he said to them, "My soul is sorrowful to the point of death. Wait here and stay awake with me." And going on a little further he fell on his face and prayed. "My Father," he said, "if it is possible, let this cup pass me by. Nevertheless, let it be as you, not I, would have it." He came back to the disciples and found them sleeping, and he said to Peter, "So you had not the strength to stay awake with me for one hour?" (NRSV)

Novena Prayer

All-knowing and surprising God,

By grace you guide us in the light of your path.

Hear us today as we bring our concerns before you . . .

[state your petitions here]

May the Lord mold our hearts in the love of God, the patience of Christ, and the warmth of the Holy Spirit. Amen.

Going to Confession

Penitence is the resurrection of character.

—FATHER ANDREW, *MEDITATIONS FOR EVERY DAY*[12]

I set to seriously practicing my spirituality only when I began to encounter what I found to be strange. Much of Catholic spirituality was strange to me at first, given where I had come from. But moving beyond tourism is essential to spiritual practice, and I began to dive headlong into what was strange to me, many years ago.

In *Redburn,* Herman Melville describes what a young whaler found when he first traveled the world aboard a whaling ship. He had expected one set of experiences but instead faced another:

> It was then, I began to see, that my prospects of seeing the world as a sailor were after all, but very doubtful; for sailors only go round the world, without going into it; and their reminiscences of travel are only a dim recollection of

> a chain of tap-rooms surrounding the globe. . . . They but touch the perimeter of the circle, hover about the edges of terra-firma; and only land upon wharfs and pier-heads.[13]

I once had a similar experience while traveling with my wife and children on a Caribbean cruise. The cruise was a gift, which is why we were going, and our other incentive was the promise in the brochure of seeing the Cayman Islands and Mexico on our calls at port. Well, if you have ever been on a cruise—particularly since 9/11—you know where this is going. Most of our ports of call were tourist traps owned by the cruise companies themselves. Not only did we not see anything of the Caymans or Mexico, but we didn't experience anything besides a beach and a plethora of preselected and prefabricated souvenirs. What a disappointment tourism can be!

A feeling of mystery is vital and vivid for Catholic spiritual practices—and they draw us to the oddest practices. The pieties or devotional practices of Catholic spirituality don't make a lot of sense in the "real" world. But these things involve us and surround us like the fog of incense at the Saturday night Easter vigil.

The first time that I went to confession, I was in another country. I was thirty-two and in London on business, and I felt safe enough that no one would know me. I could never have brought myself to enter a confessional in my hometown. It was a Friday, a popular day for the sacrament, and I cheered myself through it by thinking I was mostly curious to see if the conversation would go as it does in the movies.

The night before, I sat on my hotel room bed and began to think of what exactly I would confess to the priest. Nothing came to me. So I grabbed a pen and a notebook to stimulate the brain and prompt a list of sins. Still, nothing came. I have never believed myself perfect, but pressed for specifics, I drew a blank.

The prayer of confession that we Episcopalians intone every Sunday from the Book of Common Prayer popped into my mind at that moment. The prayer came to me in response to my interior dialogue: "Come on, Jon, you sin. God knows *you sin!*" Ah, yes, I do indeed confess; in fact, I do it every Sunday! I thought.

Here's how that Sunday prayer goes: "We confess that we have sinned against you in thought, word, and deed, by what we have done, and by what we have left undone. We have not loved you with our whole heart. We have not loved our neighbors as ourselves. And we humbly repent." But there is nothing specific at all about that, I thought to myself. In terms of going to a priest for confession, that gets me nowhere. I have to name names. I have to actually tick off stuff that I've done, not just admit that I must have done something wrong.

Jon, you are a wretch! I eventually began telling myself. A worm! Why can't you come up with evidence of what you know to be true? After an hour or so of this, I finally went to bed. It had become clear that confession was something I sorely needed. The next morning, I ended up ducking into the confessional booth with a short list of general faults and sins from years earlier because I was so out of the habit of considering my own unrighteousness.

Catholics confess their specific sins to their priest because they need to say them out loud, heal, and move on. We heal best when we allow others to help. And we cannot heal unless we can actually recall and name what we need to heal from. As G. K. Chesterton said:

> When a Catholic comes from Confession, he does truly, by definition, step out again into that dawn of his own

> beginning and look with new eyes across the world. . . . He believes that in that dim corner, and in that brief ritual, God has really remade him in His own image. He is now a new experiment of the Creator. He is as much a new experiment as he was when he was really only five years old. He stands . . . in the white light at the worthy beginning of the life of a man. The accumulations of time can no longer terrify. He may be grey and gouty; but he is only five minutes old.[14]

I do this better today than I did the first time. And I actually try to confess regularly to my Episcopal priest in Vermont. Ours may be the only regular confessional in the Episcopal church in New England. I've never heard of any others. I am beginning to be able to think more readily of my specific misdeeds and faults. My sins were always there, of course, but I had elaborately hidden them under years of general confessions and self-justifications.

The greatest mystery of Catholic spirituality is to allow there to be mystery. When you can't believe, Catholics will tell you, pray. You can't will yourself to faith; it comes from God, wells up within you, sometimes as a great surprise. You want to believe more? Then first act as if you believe. Gerard Manley Hopkins said that he converted to Catholicism because of his love for mystery. He reflected in his journal that while non-Catholics see mystery as "interesting uncertainty," Catholics understand mystery as "incomprehensible certainty"—something to trust even though it doesn't often make sense. There are lessons of confession, and the mystery of absolution that follows it as a solemn promise, and these escape us unless we actually do it, and confess.[15]

Saint Francis de Sales once said that promptness and quickness were essential components to spiritual practice done well; in *The Devout Life,* he advised, "Devotion is nothing else than spiritual agility and vivacity, by means of which charity does its work in us, or we through it, promptly and heartily." By this he meant that spiritual practices are supposed to become in us spiritual habits. The measured response becomes the quick response.

The Sacred Heart of Jesus

> Catholicism was also mystery: the competent mutter and movement of the priest at the altar, the words of power half-understood, the sense of being in touch, literally in touch, with holy things, with Holiness itself.
>
> —EAMON DUFFY, "CONFESSIONS OF A CRADLE CATHOLIC"[16]

It is unusual to think of the heart of Jesus as a thing, an object, but it is precisely that in Catholic piety. As the *Catechism* explains, "The Church has always acknowledged that in the body of Jesus 'we see our God made visible and so are caught up in love of the God we cannot see.' The individual characteristics of Christ's body express the divine person of God's Son. He has made the features of his human body his own" (para. 477).

We get tripped up by the language. That very Roman Catholic phrase "the sacred heart of Jesus" was refined only in the past three centuries and became so kitschy in the last century as to embarrass devout Mass-goers, let alone put off the rest of us. Metaphors require visible images in order for most people to digest and understand them; hence the kitsch. But images of flaming hearts, of Jesus pointing to his heart pounding out of his chest, communicate very little about the fleshiness of the heart that belonged to the incarnate Christ.

The sacred heart of Jesus of Catholic tradition begins with anatomy and then moves into metaphor. The heart is the physical organ that gives life to everything else; it is the engine of the human animal. It is also the locus of love in the human body. In the Hebrew language of first-century Judaism, "heart" meant the whole self, the human person. Then, as now, it is the place of passion.

The human animal endlessly strives to relate to the love that is waiting in the human heart. Our strivings are often misguided—focused on false things rather than true things—and so our yearnings for love are sometimes frustrated. But at other times, we exult. The point is that desire for God begins in the same place where God seeks to dwell.

Most important, the anatomical heart of human flesh became the locus of Divine love; the heart of Jesus was the expression of God's love. Again to quote the *Catechism,* "He has loved us all with a human heart. For this reason, the Sacred Heart of Jesus, pierced by our sins and for our salvation, 'is quite rightly considered the chief sign and symbol of that . . . love with which the divine Redeemer continually loves the eternal Father and all human beings' without exception" (para. 478).

Even the ancients knew that the heart was the center of the body and the entity that pumped blood throughout it. Blood was an essential metaphor for understanding the life and death of Jesus. John the Baptist called his cousin, Jesus, the Lamb of God. On the occasion when Jesus taught "I am the bread of life," he also taught that "those who eat my flesh and drink my blood have eternal life . . . for my flesh is true food and my blood is true drink." Thirty years later, Saint Paul compared him to the Passover lamb that was slain. These symbols were easily deciphered: the blood of Jesus was like the blood that God told Moses to put on the doors of the Jews' houses in Egypt so that God would pass over them and save their lives. But Jesus didn't just promise salvation from calamity; he promised eternal life—a better, eternal, manna and blood.

For those of us more accustomed to spirituality that rarely leaves our heads, the veneration of the heart of Jesus can be off-putting. And modern science has made the brain far more important than the heart. The human heart that used to love and be the center of passion—beat upon by the fists of saints who have wanted to love God more profoundly—has been replaced in our more scientific imaginations by the human brain that triggers every emotion. A heart only pumps blood.

I first encountered this reimaging as a philosophy student in college twenty years ago. In our class on epistemology (theories of knowing), we studied artificial intelligence and focused for about a week on what is called the "brain in a vat" argument. It originated in science-fiction novels. Imagine that a crazy villain kidnaps you and removes your brain. He wants you to stay alive, however. The villain places your brain in a vat of life-sustaining elements and nutrients. He then manipulates your brain by using his diabolical but detailed knowledge of how brains function, stimulating it in ways that make you feel as if you are still alive and functioning normally. Before you know any differently, "you" are walking home from work, greeting your wife, and beginning to make dinner for the kids. But is it really you doing those things? It is only your brain in the vat that tells you that you are doing those things. We have artificial intelligence to thank for virtual reality. Games and movies such as *The Matrix* rely heavily on these theories.

If right now you were simply a brain in a vat, you wouldn't know. You wouldn't know that you had been disembodied. Or would you? Are there ways in which the heart instructs us that are different from what our brains do? These are subtle areas of inquiry best left to experts. But I suspect that like the chimpanzee who dies from a lack of physical contact with its mother after birth, we would die without hearts.

I am reminded of something that the twenty-one-year-old William Butler Yeats once wrote in a letter to one of his friends at school. Yeats was complaining that a novelist he otherwise admired allowed her characters to suggest that the intellect is superior to the passions. "She is too reasonable," Yeats wrote. "I hate reasonable people, the activity of their brains sucks up all the blood out of their hearts. . . . The only business of the head in the world is to bow a ceaseless obeisance to the heart."[17] The heart learns lessons that the brain will always miss.

There are spiritual practices surrounding the adoration of the sacred heart; these are usually lumped together in what is called "devotion to the sacred heart." A Catholic will consciously share in Christ's agony in prayer, remembering the night when he was arrested, by spending an hour in prayer from 11:00 P.M. until midnight on Thursday evening before receiving Communion on the first Friday of the month. This devotion was formally approved by the Church a little more than two hundred years ago as a way of a combating heresies that had persisted since the earliest centuries of Christianity. These heretical ideas all argued so strongly for Christ's Divine nature as to exclude or severely diminish his humanness.

The purpose of any devotion to the heart of Jesus is to make your own heart more like his. Nowhere is this explained more eloquently than in Thomas Kempis' classic work, *The Imitation of Christ:*

> The Kingdom of God is within you, says the Lord. Turn with your whole heart unto the Lord, forsake this wretched world, and then your soul will find rest. Learn to despise outward things and to give yourself to things inward, and then you will perceive the Kingdom of God to come into you. For the Kingdom of God is peace and joy in the Holy Ghost, which is not given to all. Christ will come unto thee, and show you His consolation, if you prepare for Him a worthy home within you. All His glory and beauty is from within, and there He delights in Himself. He often visits the inward person and has sweet discourse, pleasant solace, much peace, and familiarity that is exceeding wonderful.[18]

Similarly, Saint Bernard of Clairvaux wrote the following prayer, which appears in many Catholic prayer books:

> How good and sweet it is, Jesus, to dwell in your heart! All my thoughts and affections will I sink in the Heart of Jesus, my Lord. I have found the Heart of my king, my brother, my friend, the Heart of my beloved Jesus. And now that I have found your Heart, which is also mine, dear Jesus, I will pray to you. Grant that my prayer may reach you, may find entrance to your Heart. Draw me to yourself. O Jesus, who is infinitely above all beauty and every charm, wash me clean from my defilement; wipe out even the smallest trace of sin. If you, who is all-pure, will purify me, I will be able to make my way into your Heart and dwell there all my life long. There I will learn to know your will, and find the grace to fulfill it. Amen.

The sacred heart of Jesus is the point where the practicality of Catholic spiritual practice—using stuff like rosary beads and little books and practices like images and novenas—meets the mystical reality of becoming a new person. All of it works together. But then there is *more* than spiritual practice, and there are reasons why some Catholic devotions feel extravagant in their mystical overtones. One Desert Father, Abba Lot, once visited another, Abba Joseph, and asked him where else he could go and what else he could do to deepen his spiritual practice. Abba Lot said, "I say the Divine Office. I fast. I pray. I meditate. I live peacefully with my neighbors. I help others. What else is there?" As the story goes, Abba Joseph stood up and stretched his arms and hands to the sky. His long fingers appeared even longer to Abba Lot, and they became ten lamps of fire, as if volts were leaving the abba's body. "If you are willing, you can become all flame!" he said.

SECTION FIVE

MY OWN CLOUD OF WITNESSES

Thomas Merton

Is it an accident when friends and strangers introduce you to one writer, teacher, or practitioner rather than another? Where does the wisdom come from that leads people to place signposts along your way? Life is pilgrimage in ways that we rarely ever realize.

In the Gospel story of the road to Emmaus (Luke 24:13–32), the scene is Easter Sunday morning, the very day of the Resurrection. The tomb has already been found empty. The Marys found it first and spoke with two angels beside the stone that had been rolled away. They immediately went to tell the disciples, and the men thought they were crazy. "This story of theirs seemed pure nonsense, and they did not believe them," the text says. And so Peter, the boldest, ran himself to the tomb and found no body there. He was amazed but still did not know what was happening.

"Now that very same day . . . ," the story begins, two men who were keeping a low profile since the Crucifixion "were on their way to a village called Emmaus, seven miles from Jerusalem." This village no longer exists but could have been what is today known as el-Qubeibeh. The identity of only one of the men is told in the story: Cleopas, called Clopas in John's Gospel, the husband of one of the Marys.

As the two men were talking about the events of recent days, "Jesus himself came up and walked by their side; but their eyes were prevented from recognizing him." They were so preoccupied and sad that seeing what was right in front of them became temporarily impossible. When Jesus asks, "What are all these things that you are discussing?" Cleopas actually responds cuttingly, "You must be the only person staying in Jerusalem who does not know the things that have been happening there these last few days." And then Cleopas tells Jesus of their disappointment in Jesus, explaining, "Our own hope had been that he would be the one to set Israel free."

Still unknown to the men, Jesus begins to explain the prophets and all that they said about the coming of the Messiah and tells them, "You foolish men! So slow to believe!" But they still do not see him. As "they drew near to the village to which they were going, he made as if to go on; but they pressed him to stay." They sat down together at a meal prepared by an innkeeper.

> Now while he was with them at table, he took the bread and said the blessing; then he broke it and handed it to them. And their eyes were opened and they recognized him; but he had vanished from their sight. Then they said to each other, "Did not our hearts burn within us as he talked to us on the road and explained the scriptures to us?" (NRSV)

I have found that that is precisely what happens when I follow the strands of listening to the teachers that are put in my way. My heart burns within me—not because I understand simply and clearly or because I even pick up immediately on what is important but because coming to understand is painfully slow.

Mennonites turned me on to Thomas Merton while I was a teenager. I had questions that my own pastor could not answer when it came time for me to register with the Selective Service when I turned eighteen. "Why would it be right for me to kill another human being if Jesus told his disciples to 'turn the other cheek'?" I had asked my pastor, and he didn't have a very good answer. And so I began attending meetings at the Mennonite church a few towns over.

But I didn't stop at Merton's writings on war, justice, and peace. I went back to the beginning and read his youthful autobiography, *The Seven Storey Mountain*. Merton was brash and arrogant. He was fun and smart. His parents were painters, and he spent more time in Manhattan and Europe than anywhere else in the United States. Merton graduated from Columbia University and was a "big man on campus," to be sure. But when he finally figured out who he really was, he became a monk in a remote monastery in the hills of Kentucky.

In the summer of 1941, a few months before he became a monk, Merton was living in upstate New York teaching English at Saint Bonaventure College. He was in his twenties and trying to figure out what to do with his life, attracted as he was to both the life of the mind (as a writer) and the life of the spirit (a possible religious vocation). He was debating many things within himself: Should he become a writer? Is it possible to be a writer without becoming full of oneself? What about the call to contemplation that he felt deep inside?

These tensions made Merton's life and work relevant to millions of readers, even long after his death in 1968. Many of us bump up against these same questions—not necessarily because we are writers, as he was, but because we seek to exercise our talents without self-aggrandizement. To use the language of monastic spirituality, how do we dismantle our "false self" and gradually discover our "true self" as we succeed in our work in the world? This question filled Merton with anxiety throughout his life.

His autobiography was published when Merton was only thirty-three years old. He found it nearly impossible not to write about what was happening inside of him throughout his life as a cloistered monk. And that was odd. Why would a monk—a man who has taken many vows including a vow of silence—publish? During his first visit as a retreatant to the Abbey of Gethsemane in Kentucky, during Holy Week of 1941, he wrote in his journal, "I should tear out all the other pages of this book and all the other pages of everything else I ever wrote, and begin here." In the years to follow, after hundreds of thousands of copies of *The Seven Storey Mountain* were purchased and read around the world, Merton would go through times when he wanted to stop writing altogether. He once wrote, "An author in a Trappist monastery is like a duck in a chicken coop. And he would give anything in the world to be a chicken instead of a duck." But still he wrote and expressed himself to millions of people beside his monastic brothers. These were times when he felt his ego growing faster than his spirit. But thank God, they were short-lived, and he went back to his typewriter.

He was a Catholic in the broadest of all possible meanings of the word. The essence of Merton's genius is also the reason why Merton's writings will outlive those of almost every other spiritual writer of the twentieth century. He taught those of us outside the monastery how to live more as if we were inside the monastery. He distilled the monastic life down to the point where it seemed possible to replicate it in the secular world. Before Merton, monasticism seemed to be a life of retreat, irrelevant scholarship, and prejudice against the world. After Merton, to live like a monk became synonymous with mindfulness, attentiveness, contemplation, and embracing of others.

Thomas Merton, pray for me.

Saint Francis of Assisi

I cannot really explain why or how he became the saint that speaks most directly to me, but I feel a close relationship with Francis of Assisi and have so since high school. His youthful rebellion and arguments with his father made perfect sense to me. As a teenager, Francis had to struggle to figure out the difference between what his parents wanted for him and what he wanted for himself. Once he realized that God was his real father, Francis's overearnest commitment to faith made sense to me, too. And then his forthright manner, combined with a personal gentleness, became my ideal. I learn from Francis's example and his teachings, and I consciously try to become more like him. I love the ways in which he was peaceful but not passive, loving but not always lovable.

Francis of Assisi brought light into the darkness of the later Middle Ages. He was, in the words of Dante, the "Morning Star," the sun that rises in the east to shine new light upon the dawn. Francis's life was full of poetry, both lived and spoken. His greatest biographer, Paul Sabatier, goes so far as to say, "The sermon to the birds and the first Blessing of the Animals closed the reign of Byzantine art and of the thought of which it was the image. It is the end of dogmatism and authority. Uncertainty became permissible in some small measure. It marks a date in the history of the human conscience."[1]

The century before Francis Bernardone was born in Assisi, Italy, in 1170 was one of the most corrupt in the history of the Christian Church. It was so bad in those days that it was often said the majority of priests and bishops were practicing simony (extorting money), keeping prostitutes, or doing both. The situation in France and Italy was such that it could not even be covered up. The good elements of the Church leadership felt that the pope must deal severely with the negative elements, but they feared that his sanctions would be so sweeping as to induce the faithful into the heresy of Donatism, a rejection of the Church because of some bad elements in it.

Nevertheless, in several encyclicals published between 1074 and 1109, Pope Gregory VII told all Christians that they must reject the sacraments given from the hands of corrupt priests. These letters sent out into the parishes and read aloud in public squares caused riots. This was the Middle Ages, and the Church stood at the center of public life. Religion—which was only Christianity in these communities—was not a private affair but a series of public pieties and obligations, all of which ran through the Church and the local priest for their authority.

It was into these troubled and confusing times that Francis was born. I will not outline his life story for you, here. Read G. K. Chesterton's life of Francis or Julien Green's *God's Fool* or *The Road to Assisi* by Paul Sabatier. All of them will give you a good understanding of the little poor man who became known to the world as Saint Francis.

It is his spirit that I still cling to, and I am not alone. Millions of people pray to Francis for peace; his legacy was one of peace, and even though he didn't actually pen that famous prayer, "Lord, Make Me an Instrument of Peace" (it was written anonymously just a century ago), it is full of his spirit. The stories of the wolf of Gubbio and the preaching to the birds are not just fanciful tales but part of the chronicle of Francis's extraordinary life. Sometimes saints make extraordinary things appear ordinary. We can learn from their examples that transformations of matter through the power of spirit are within our grasp too.

Francis knew inner doubt and conflict. He often wondered whether or not his life—wandering around the hilltop towns of Umbria, preaching the Good News, caring for lepers, talking with and caring for animals—was really God's work or some sort of ruse. I love him for that. I too try to do what God is asking me to do (as I attempt to figure out what that might actually be), and I am always doubting myself. You might not know it to look at me, though. I pray to Francis in my own moments of self-doubt, asking him to help me have clarity of vision and to see God at work around me and in others.

His feast day is October 4. He did not die that day so much as he was born anew on that day. His devotion to the Virgin Mary was great, and wherever heaven is to be found, Francis is praying for us there. He is not only praying for peace but urging us on toward it. And he is singing the Angelus. The name, Angelus, comes from the first word of the Annunciation story in Latin: *Angelus Domini nuntiavit Mariae* ("The angel of the Lord declared unto Mary"). The Angelus is an ancient celebration of the Incarnation and the Annunciation—the occasion when Gabriel first told Mary that she was with child. It includes these two concluding prayers: "Pour forth, we beseech thee, O Lord, Thy grace into our hearts, that we to whom the Incarnation of Christ Thy Son was made known by the message of an angel, may be His Passion and Cross be brought to the glory of His Resurrection. Through the same Christ our Lord. Amen." and "May God's help be us always, and may the souls of the faithful departed, through the mercy of God rest in peace. Amen."

Francis of Assisi, pray for me.

Every Idealist Who Has Ever Tried

There is something profoundly sad about the life of Francis of Assisi. Eight or nine years before his death, he lost control of his own movement. This was before anyone was called a "Franciscan." Francis had started simply; he heard Christ tell him to rebuild his church, and Francis took it literally to heart; he began gathering stones and learned masonry. He read the passage in the Gospels about giving your cloak to the poor, and then he went out and found a poor man with whom he could exchange clothes. Francis's father was a clothier, and so his fine garments were quite a gift! But within a decade of his first turning the world upside down with his radical commitment to the way of Jesus, Francis lost control of the movement he set in motion.

Francis didn't intend to start a movement; he only wanted to follow Christ as the Gospels explained, and he was delighted to find men and women who wanted to do the same thing. But eventually, some of those who joined him insisted that changes be made to bring the Franciscan way more in line with other monastic movements. The original ideal was lost, and Francis knew it.

There's a pattern to this sort of thing. Throughout history, we see spiritual ferment bubble up and then become institutionalized in ways that too often end the spirit of what was begun. The biologist David Sloan Wilson quotes John Wesley, the eighteenth-century founder of Methodism, as an example of how evolutionary theory relates to the alternating institution, reform, and institution of religion: "I do not see how it is possible, in the nature of things, for any revival of religion to continue for long. For religion must necessarily produce both industry and frugality. And these cannot but produce riches. But as riches increase, so will pride, anger, and love of the world in all its branches."[2] Francis of Assisi grasped this reality during his own lifetime—but that doesn't make idealists any less necessary.

Every place and time has idealists walking around. They are usually dismissed, particularly today. Basil Pennington—a Trappist monk like Thomas Merton—was just such an idealist. He believed that monks were supposed to earnestly desire to live the Rule of Saint Benedict. In other words, they were supposed to strive to be joyful in every moment, work diligently even at the meanest tasks, and pray unceasingly in the ways outlined in that medieval text. But for his attempt to do all of that, he was occasionally dismissed by his fellow monks. They sometimes felt that Basil wasn't real or at least wasn't honest because he talked of ideals. But the opposite was true. He is most real and honest who tries harder to do what is ideal than to do what is necessary.

The idealists of the first century were the ones who believed that Jesus was coming imminently again. The *Didache* is a first-century text that was discovered a little more than a hundred years ago. It is also sometimes called *The Teaching of the Twelve Apostles* because it contains the earliest writings that are not included in the New Testament canon. Toward the end, it urges the young Christian to "watch over your life. Your lamps must not go out, nor your loins ever be ungirded. On the contrary, be ready always. You do not know the hour in which Our Lord is coming."[3] I'm sure that these writers were thought to be too severe or too serious, too.

The old adage is that idealism is something one grows out of. It wears off. But there are many exceptions. Jack Kerouac, author of *On the Road,* was a Catholic idealist throughout his life, inspired with vision and imagination. "From childhood until death, Kerouac wrote letters to God, prayers to Jesus, poems to Saint Paul, and psalms to his own salvation." He even redefined the Beat movement after a religious experience he had before a statue of the Virgin Mary in a church in Lowell, Massachusetts. For Kerouac, Beat stood for "beatific."[4] He once mused, "What thoughts Jesus must have had before he 'opened his mouth' on the Mount and spoke his sermon, what long dark silent thoughts!" One of his psalm-meditations included "Like steel I will be, God, growing harder in the forge-fires, grimmer, harder, better. . . . Strike me and I will ring like a bell!"[5]

Every idealist who has ever tried is in my corner rooting me on. I believe that the devout and God-fearing person is a better human being than the sarcastic, the cynical, the intellectual, the clever, and the incredulous. I have been those other things. My rebellions have always been of the too-clever sort. I might read something that convinces me absolutely, for half an hour, that some aspect of faith or belief is for suckers. I used to believe that I knew everything, and yet I actually knew nothing. Give me simplicity of heart, God, more than cleverness. I love how Catholic spirituality brings out the idealist in me.

You've got to love the losers! Jesus didn't just honor them because he felt sorry for them; he held them up as an example for others. The idealist who actually takes the Beatitudes seriously is also one who will be ridiculed in most places today. Blessed are the poor in spirit, the gentle, those who mourn, those who are merciful, the pure in heart, the peacemakers, the persecuted—in our parlance, the losers. The kingdom of heaven is theirs.

Charles de Foucauld was born into an aristocratic family in France and served as a soldier but then decided to live among poor Muslims in North Africa. He had no followers when he was murdered in the desert in Algeria in 1916, but that didn't matter to him. He was following Christ as he believed he was supposed to. He wrote in his journal soon before he died:

> I should carry on in myself the life of Jesus: think his thoughts, repeat his words, his actions. May it be he that lives in me. I must be the image of Our Lord in his hidden life: I must proclaim, by my life, the Gospel from the rooftops. *Veni*. My courage must be equal to my will. "Seek thyself in me. Seek me in thyself." "It is time to love God." Seek God only. Kindness. Gentleness. Sweetness. Courage. Humility.[6]

De Foucauld is an example of the hidden saint, the idealist Catholic who saves the world quietly in prayer and witness.

Pray for me, Charles de Foucauld.

G. K. Chesterton

If there was ever to be a patron saint of Catholic converts, it would probably *not* be G. K. Chesterton—at least not today. Chesterton lacked the certainty of today's converts. And he was too full of mirth to be taken seriously. Franz Kafka once remarked, "He is so happy! One might almost believe he had found God."[7] Another critic and friend of his correctly characterized Chesterton's spirituality as a "mysticism of happiness."[8]

Many of Chesterton's contemporaries in the Roman Catholic Church were more than wary of his optimism. They believed that he lacked a serious appreciation of what faith means in a life. Chesterton was an optimistic lover of people. Some of his contemporaries, such as the French novelist Léon Bloy and the English poet Francis Thompson, focused on the dark side of human nature and emphasized the pain and oppression of everyday life in contrast to the glory of the hereafter. But for the enormous Chesterton (he loved to eat), the hereafter was foretold in the happiness of daily living. He was to Catholic faith what Walt Whitman was to humanism.

These sorts of differences in outlook are often the result of personality rather than theology. Anne Enright—one of today's most interesting Irish novelists—recently described her daughter by saying, "The child has what might be called a religious temperament, being prone to bliss and rendered solemn by the sacred"—in contrast to her other child—"Her brother is a much more pragmatic, ironic sort of guy. He doesn't believe or disbelieve things as much as look at them to see what they might do next."[9] I can see these sorts of dispositional differences in my own kids. Such traits don't determine our spiritual outlook, but they certainly dispose us differently. Chesterton was an extrovert to the greatest degree. He loved to talk and debate, and he counted among his friends many of the most interesting public figures of the early twentieth century. Chesterton saw the dark side of human nature as something to be overcome by Christ, never as something sinister that was somehow overwhelming. He came to his conversion through many of the isms that plagued the last century: modernism, materialism, Marxism, determinism.

Chesterton makes everything seem so clear. The Catholic faith is full of blessed, big ideas, and Chesterton's books—whether on Thomas Aquinas, Francis of Assisi, Orthodoxy, or dozens of other topics—contain the most succinct and summarizing prose in our language. He converted to Catholicism as a young man after having written a book titled *Heretics;* some critics told him he should write his next book about what he does believe rather than what he does not. The classic *Orthodoxy* was the result, and so was Chesterton's baptism into the Roman Catholic Church.

Chesterton makes it simple to see Christ clearly. And it is no wonder that his writings have ushered many a Christian into the Catholic Church. He once wrote the following in his *Autobiography,* recounting a conversation he had with a friend:

> He once made to me the very sensible remark, "The only little difficulty that I have about joining the

> Catholic Church is that I do not think I believe in God. All the rest of the Catholic system is so obviously right and so obviously superior to anything else, that I cannot imagine anyone having any doubt about it." And I remember that he was grimly gratified when I told him, at a later stage of my own beliefs, that real Catholics are intelligent enough to have this difficulty; and that St. Thomas Aquinas practically begins his whole argument by saying, "Is there a God? Apparently not." But, I added, it was my experience that entering into the system even socially brought an ever-increasing certitude upon the original question.[10]

Chesterton's Catholicism is full of enthusiasm for an earlier time. When he writes of yearning for what is Catholic, he is saying that he wants to submit to the oldest and soundest ecclesiastical footing he can find: the tradition of Saint Peter and Rome. The meaning of Catholic faith, according to Chesterton, is humility. He expresses this best in his fiction, through the detective-priest character of Father Brown:

> "I think there is something rather dangerous about standing on these high places even to pray," said Father Brown. "Heights were made to be looked at, not to be looked from."
>
> "Do you mean that one may fall over?" asked Wilfred.
>
> "I mean that one's soul may fall if one's body doesn't," said the other priest.
>
> "I scarcely understand you," remarked Bohun indistinctly.
>
> "Look at that blacksmith, for instance," went on Father Brown calmly: "a good man, but not a Christian—hard, imperious, unforgiving. Well, his Scotch religion was made up by men who prayed on hills and high crags, and learnt to look down on the world more than to

> look up at heaven. Humility is the mother of giants. One sees great things from the valley; only small things from the peak."[11]

He believed that logic is essential to thinking clearly but also that logic does not explain all that we may think. To be Catholic is to be defined, in many ways and on many subjects, by revelation. He emphasized that faith makes believers; believers don't make faith. Chesterton defines orthodoxy—a subject about which he was very interested—as an evolving community and tradition that enables one to be free in Christ and full of happiness. Throughout his life and writings, he infects me with a joy that comes in moving beyond the details. He explains:

> This is the thrilling romance of Orthodoxy. People have fallen into a foolish habit of speaking of orthodoxy as something heavy, humdrum, and safe. There never was anything so perilous or so exciting as orthodoxy. . . . The Church in its early days went fierce and fast with any warhorse. . . . She swerved to left and right, so as exactly to avoid enormous obstacles. . . . The orthodox Church never took the tame course or accepted the conventions; the orthodox Church was never respectable. It would have been easier to have accepted the earthly power of the Arians. It would have been easy, in the Calvinistic seventeenth century, to fall into the bottomless pit of predestination. It is easy to be a madman: it is easy to be a heretic. . . . To have fallen into any one of the fads from Gnosticism to Christian Science would indeed have been obvious and tame. But to have avoided them all has been one whirling adventure; and in my vision the heavenly chariot flies thundering through the ages, the dull heresies sprawling and prostrate, the wild truth reeling but erect.[12]

Almost everything is too small for Chesterton. Orthodoxy is vast. To be Catholic is to be vast. Our potential for happiness is enormous. When asked by the venerable *Times* of London to contribute to a series of essays on the theme, "What's Wrong with the World?" Chesterton wrote the following:

Dear Sirs,
I am.

Sincerely yours,
G. K. Chesterton

He didn't take himself too seriously, and he certainly didn't take ponderous intellectuals very seriously either. He wrote like a percussionist: making loud, piercing sounds from the back row. But Chesterton was also making a serious point in this little statement: human sinfulness is real, and Chesterton's own nature was a piece of the biggest problem for the world.

Chesterton, pray for me.

Flannery O'Connor

Catholic novelists often seem to have names that are difficult to forget. Their names can easily shorten into one-word monikers: Liam—as in Callanan (*The Cloud Atlas*)—and Chimamanda—as in Ngozi Adichie (*Purple Hibiscus*), two contemporary authors of best-sellers, come immediately to mind. And then there are Muriel Spark, Graham Greene, and Walker Percy from a couple of decades ago. They have all taught me much about what it means to be human and Catholic, but none so much as Flannery—as in O'Connor.

A high school English teacher taught me to love the stories of Flannery O'Connor. He saw in her writing a stubborn perspective on truth that would appeal to teenagers trying to navigate the world of false self—and he was right. We devoured her stories.

There is no doubt that religion is strange both to those of us on the inside of it and to those looking in from outside. Practicing religion can be a strange exercise. O'Connor thought that we were made for this sort of strangeness.

"We're all grotesque," she once wrote in answer to a question about why her characters were always odd, often even physically disfigured. Not only was O'Connor intrigued by the rough side of humanity, but she was also adept at drawing characters who magnified the darkness of being human apart from God.

She grew up in rural Georgia as an only child. Her father died of lupus, an autoimmune disease that occasionally runs in families, when O'Connor was still a teenager. She also developed the disease, which gradually ravaged her body until her own premature death at the age of thirty-nine in 1964. O'Connor remained close to her mother, and they lived together on the family farm in the middle of Georgia for most of O'Connor's life. She never married. They were devout Catholics living in the heart of the evangelical Protestant American South. From her earliest years, O'Connor knew that much about her life was unusual compared to others around her.

She once expressed her admiration for a local pastor who pinned a real lamb to a wooden cross and then slaughtered it before the eyes of his congregation. She believed that the Protestant pastor understood the Mass in ways that were lost on many of her fellow Catholics.

O'Connor writes not about grotesque and ugly characters but about the grotesque and ugly parts of all of us. She writes about what needs forgiving in human life. And when we face it—like taking distasteful medicine—we see the real begin to shatter our structured imaginings of how we'd rather see ourselves.

She felt that it was necessary to write in ways that were shocking. She once said, "When you can assume that your audience holds the same beliefs you do, you can relax a little and use more normal ways of talking to it; when you have to assume that it does not, then you have to make your vision apparent by shock—to the hard of hearing you shout, and for the almost-blind you draw large and startling figures."[13]

The images that we construct for God are torn down in O'Connor's stories. We may see God as big and kindly, strong and comforting, warm and supportive, like an unconditional friend. But O'Connor shows us other sides to the Divine-human relationship. The Christian becomes the material in a sculptor's hands. The sculptor will lop off and then chip away as he sees fit. We don't like that. Our God has become domesticated almost like a dog on a leash. We imagine God's responses and accommodations of our sins before we even commit them. God has so often become the spoonful of sugar before the medicine even goes down. She explains, "My own feeling is that writers who see by the light of their Christian faith will have, in these times, the sharpest eyes for the grotesque, for the perverse, and for the unacceptable. . . . Redemption is meaningless unless there is cause for it in the actual life we live, and for the last few centuries there has been operating in our culture the secular belief that there is no such cause."[14]

The American South of Flannery's stories is replete with sacraments. In her story "The River," a drowning becomes the sacrament of Baptism. In various other tales, small and everyday acts of violence become means of grace. Her point in all of this is to refute the anti-Catholic heresy that sees the world as dualistic. Various dualist groups over the centuries—including much of today's spiritual writing—have argued that the earth, the material or created world, is somehow a necessarily evil, while the spiritual world, which fights against it from without rather than from within, is inherently good. And so, the theory goes, the more spiritual we become, the more we are able to remove ourselves from the world.

In the sacramental world that Flannery O'Connor creates, her Catholic imagination constructs characters that encounter grace right in the middle of what is considered most material and base. Grace is impossible, in an O'Connor story, apart from what we encounter in and through our bodies, in the midst of the mess, but even more important, the darkness of life.

Consider the character of Rufus Johnson in the story "The Lame Shall Enter First." He is a fourteen-year-old troubled boy with a clubfoot from a broken home, raised by a mostly absent grandfather. Rufus has just recently been released from the reformatory home, where he was sentenced for various petty crimes. He eats out of garbage cans and reads the Bible enough to believe that the devil has control over his soul.

Contrast Rufus with a man named Sheppard (aptly named, as many of O'Connor's characters are) who is the classic bleeding-heart liberal. Sheppard is a widower who spent the last year counseling with Rufus in the reformatory, and he believes he can help change Rufus's life for the better. Sheppard seems to actually relish the low place that Rufus finds himself in. He attempts to shock his own ten-year-old son out of his laziness by telling him, "Rufus's father died before he was born. . . . His mother is in the state penitentiary. He was raised by his grandfather in a shack without water or electricity and the old man beat him every day. How would you like to belong to a family like that?"

Sheppard wants Rufus to come and live with him and his son. Wanting Rufus to become educated, he urges him not to believe in spiritual things and tells him, "Maybe I can explain your devil to you." Sheppard wants to help Rufus, but his assistance is entirely secular. The narrator of the tale tells of the counselor's fantasy about getting legal custody of the boy, and explains: "Nothing excited [Sheppard] so much as thinking what he could do for such a boy. First he would have him fitted for a new orthopedic shoe. . . . Then he would encourage him in some particular intellectual interest."

Throughout "The Lame Shall Enter First," Rufus remains what most of us would call a "bad kid," and Sheppard goes out of his way to try and make a better life for the troubled boy. Sheppard is the model of intelligence, and Rufus is simply bad.

The climax comes after many conflicts between Rufus and Sheppard, toward the end, when Sheppard comes home to find Rufus and his son, Norton, on the couch together discussing heaven and hell while reading a Bible that Rufus has stolen from a local store. Sheppard is disgusted by all of this. "Stop talking this nonsense," he says to them. "That book is something for you to hide behind. . . . It's for cowards, people who are afraid to stand on their own feet and figure things out for themselves." Sheppard challenges Rufus, trying finally to teach him how to think for himself, telling him that he doesn't actually believe what he is reading:

> "I ain't too intelligent," the boy muttered. "You don't know nothing about me. Even if I didn't believe it, it would still be true. . . . I believe it!" Johnson said breathlessly. "I'll show you I believe it!" He opened the book in his lap and tore out a page of it and thrust it into his mouth. He fixed his eyes on Sheppard. His jaws worked furiously and the paper crackled as he chewed it.
>
> "Stop this," Sheppard said in a dry, burnt-out voice. "Stop it."

O'Connor forces us to see light in darkness and from strange angles. What is false or bad often appears to be real and good. Revelation is everywhere. There is always something eternal lurking around us, and the more polished we are, sometimes, the poorer is our ability to see it. The climactic scene concludes:

> "I've eaten it!" the boy cried. Wonder transformed his face. "I've eaten it like Ezekiel and I don't want none of your food after it nor no more ever."
>
> "Go then," Sheppard said softly. "Go. Go."
>
> The boy rose and picked up the Bible and started toward the hall with it. At the door he paused, a small black figure on the threshold of some dark apocalypse. "The devil has you in his power," he said in a jubilant voice and disappeared.

Flannery O'Connor was intrigued by how rarely we see Jesus spend time with nice, sophisticated, decent, upper-middle-class, religious people. There is a falsity to such lives that the Gospels often throw into clearer light. Instead, we more often see Jesus explaining and handing out grace to the types he does hang out with: tax collectors, prostitutes, the sick, the flawed, the rejected, and the ones who have to work so hard to make a living that they don't have time to study the scriptures in the temple. The well-behaved and respectable were the people who most angered Jesus because they were fooling themselves and others. Instead, Jesus thanked people like Rufus, regardless of how they appeared on the outside, saying, "So if anyone declares himself for me in the presence of human beings, I will declare myself for him in the presence of my Father in heaven" (Matthew 10:32).

Two verses later, Jesus offers what best explains the odd way that grace seems to work in O'Connor's stories: "Do not suppose that I have come to bring peace to the earth: it is not peace I have come to bring, but a sword" (Matthew 10:34). Like the sword in Jesus' metaphor, real grace—to truly follow in Christ's footsteps—is to be hurt, to bleed, to be maimed. Clubfeet and twisted lips are only outward signs in O'Connor's stories of the sort of twisting that is inside of us. We assume—and why wouldn't we, given the prevailing teachings of evangelical prosperity gospel preachers—that the closer we follow Jesus, the prettier we will become, the wealthier we will become, and the more friends we will have. Jesus says the opposite.

Flannery O'Connor, pray for me.

The *Catechism* as a Mystical Novel

> There is no human being on earth who is capable of declaring who he is . . . or what his real *name* is, his imperishable Name in the registry of Light. . . . History is an immense liturgical text, where the *i*'s and the periods are not worth less than the versicles or whole chapters, but the importance of both is undeterminable and is profoundly hidden.
>
> —LÉON BLOY, *L'AME DE NAPOLÉON*[15]

The Zohar is the most basic and classical text of Jewish spirituality or kabbalah. It is also somewhat bizarre and confusing, combining commentary on the first five books of the Bible (the Torah) with symbolism, layers of terminology developed over centuries by clerics, and the framework of a mystical narrative. The hero of the Zohar is a rabbi, the disciple of another rabbi, who lives in the land known today as Israel, sometime around the second century after Christ.

I believe that what the Zohar is to Judaism, the *Catechism of the Catholic Church* is for Christians. I have quoted from the

Catechism many times already in this book, but it is much more than a book of teachings and quotes. Like the Zohar, the *Catechism* is really a mystical novel. Combining a great narrative (storytelling, fiction, and myth all at once), mystical nuance, and a weaving together of all reasons for living, this fat little book is both difficult and important. It is a repository that is at once beautiful and unusual.

Imagine an ancient church in a holy city that stands out among all of the buildings around it. The architecture soars, but not so high that it seems garish. The doors to the sanctuary remain almost continuously open, tied back with knotted cords, and are almost as old as the bricks of the street.

The cellar of this basilica intrigues archaeologists, for the underground corridors are seemingly endless and intricate, full of historical meaning and secret passages. Some of the rooms in these caverns have stood empty for centuries, full of treasures both documented and undiscovered. Other rooms more closely resemble burial grounds, leaving the observer to wonder what lies underneath. Beneath layers of cement, wood, and gravel may be treasures there that are akin to long-forgotten species, and there is also an underbelly of the gratefully forgotten or the intentionally discarded.

In the nave of this imaginary church, the observer's eye is drawn away from a resplendent altar to hundreds of chapels lining the aisles. In these sacred, lonely places, the spirits of heroes stand by. As valuable books were once chained to the desks in medieval scriptoria, these saintly men and women linger beyond the aisles of the great cathedral, keeping watch like lit candles.

There is a library in the old church as well. Shelves stand floor to ceiling, but then there are gaps in the floor and stairs spiraling downward, with more shelves along their wings. Books pile in corners and stack sometimes neatly on thick wooden desks. Some of the volumes are well thumbed, others have uncut pages, and still others are not books at all but rolls, dating to the centuries before the church was born. You can see, upon opening any book, that people of different eras have written in the margins their own thoughts about the passages, arguing with them, refining them. Sitting nearby, you see that in later published editions of the same books, these marginalia have been included. There seems to be no end to the commentary on the life of God.

The *Catechism of the Catholic Church* is a living monument similar to the imaginary one that I have just described. Behind the dogmatic phrasings and proof-texting that fills its 864 pages is the Person to which that great nave points us. The layers of discussion are rich like cake, even though they represent witnesses to faith almost entirely Western or Middle Eastern, from eras long ago.

Reading the *Catechism* is not exactly like reading the Zohar. The *Catechism* is not as overtly inventive as the Zohar, but it has the same sort of poetry that mixes with a subtle narrative drive. Christ is the hero of the *Catechism,* and humanity is the subject.

A *catechism* is "a summary of principles, often in question-and-answer format," according to Webster's. This *Catechism* offers four "pillars of faith" that are requirements of belief: the Nicene Creed, the Ten Commandments, the Seven Sacraments, and the "Our Father." Each is explained in detail. Catechisms have been used to instruct believers in the points of faith for millennia, but assigning them the word *catechism* is rather new. It was Martin Luther who first used the term to describe both the short and long versions of his own revised handbook of the basic essentials of faith; Luther's *Short Catechism* is considered his literary masterpiece.

Catechetical instruction has grown over two thousand years. Like an ancient tree, its roots are well established, but there is always a tiny bit of new growth from century to century on the outer branches. The current, massive little book known as the *Catechism of the Catholic Church* was published in 1992, not long ago. It appeared first in French and Latin and was translated into English by 1997, when it immediately became a best-seller in every English-speaking country in the world. This tome is divided into four parts that may be described this way:

1. We believe: the scriptures and the creeds
2. We celebrate: the liturgy, mysteries, and sacraments
3. We do: the Christian way of life, including happiness, virtue, passion, conscience, and the commandments
4. We pray: vocal prayer, meditation, contemplation, the prayer of the worldwide Church, and the Lord's Prayer

Human beings are the subject, more than God. The authors are anonymous, in the way that the authors of a Wikipedia article are unsung: sometimes identified but usually behind the scenes. This great novel may best be described as "wikicatechism."

To know God is to live in eternity and—this is the subterfuge of the entire story—such knowledge is possible right in front of you, on the very page you are reading, in the very sentence you are reading right now, in the *Catechism*. The beginning of the book is the beginning of the story is the beginning of your life, if you enter into this novel with your entire self. Think of it all as like a virtual reality story into which you stand and experience everything that is real rather than virtual. Don't be beguiled by the fact that there are words on a page, reminding you of many pages of words that you have nodded off while reading before. This is the story of eternal salvation, and you are in the middle of it already!

The story unfolds; what is for you now is as it was for others long ago: "In the beginning, God . . ." has many meanings. Before we all began, God created humanity. Why? Because he wanted to share in the blessing of life. Why would God want to be alone? It is *that* we even exist, not *why* we exist, that is the most remarkable mystery of all.

But there are problems in the *Catechism*. As in any great book, there are controversial elements and occasional places where the great cathedral needs to consider removing some more things to the basement. For instance, the section on blasphemy, a grave sin, includes "words of . . . reproach, or defiance" against God (para. 2147). Reproach and defiance are often markers of real faith, which, when mingled with doubt, makes for the best of believers.

In the section headed "The Vocation to Chastity," few today will appreciate the paragraphs on "offenses against chastity" where sexual pleasure sought for its own sake (defined as lust) and masturbation are put on a par with pornography and rape. Sometimes the Church offers official teaching in areas that would best be left to others. The section that follows—"The Love of Husband and Wife"—is more representative of how poetry and wisdom and odd traditions mingle in the *Catechism*. The talk of evil and immortality in contraception has grown tiresome, lampooned in the novels of David Lodge and in reminders from stubborn popes. Nevertheless, what a mystical thing "the fecundity of marriage" is! Read *that*—the beautiful stuff of catechisms!

A much earlier catechism known as the Roman Catechism of the Council of Trent (sixteenth century), summarized beautifully:

> The whole concern of doctrine and its teaching must be directed to the love that never ends. Whether something is proposed for belief, for hope or for action, the love of our Lord must always be made accessible, so that anyone can see that all the works of perfect Christian virtue spring from love and have no other objective than to arrive at love.

This wikicatechism is not only a mystical novel but also a living demonstration that the ancient faith itself is "wikicatholicism."

SECTION SIX

TOGETHER WITH OTHERS

Take Me to the River

> The Holy Catholic Church looks more like the five thousand whom the Lord fed on the hillside than she does the small group of insiders in the Upper Room.
>
> —Thomas Howard, *Lead, Kindly Light*[1]

Readers who are near my age of forty will probably remember playing Pac-Man. We played it on large tables, roughly the size of a 1950s hi-fi or television console that was made to look like a piece of furniture. I loved Pac-Man. You moved a lever left and right, up and down, to control the movement of your Pac-Man through a maze, intent on eating all of the little dots that he came upon and avoiding the opposing Pac-Men. I especially loved it when I was able to gobble up the dancing cherries that floated up and down the corridors of the Pac-Man's domain. They were worth extra points, which never really concerned me. Instead, I liked what happened next: you'd gobble the cherries and then miraculously become invincible. A glow of light surrounded your Pac-Man body. You were blessed with superspeed. And you were suddenly—and fleetingly—able to rush around the maze and not only snatch up the little white dots but also catch up with and consume the other assorted fruit that were worth the big points.

I used to wish that life were like those Pac-Man moments. We'd be able to chomp down magical fruit that allows us to speed past everyone else and, most of all, never be hurt. Not even touched. Wouldn't that be the ideal? Of course not—I know that now. Life is painful and is better for it. I have experienced how the most painful moments become the most blessed.

The *Penny Catechism* of Catholic Sunday school classes a century ago posed in its question and answer number 340:

> *How are we to love one another?*
> We are to love one another by wishing well to one another, and praying for one another; and by never allowing ourselves any thought, word or deed to the injury of anyone.

We would no longer accept that explanation today, would we? Loving one another involves far more than good intentions and avoiding doing wrong. To love is to act. If for no other reason, *that* is why I go to church. That is why being almost Catholic, for me, has to be more than spirituality by myself.

Spiritual practice is private but shared; it is intensely personal but common. The inevitable result of spiritual practice is spiritual experience, things like "conversations with the unseen, voices and visions, responses to prayer, changes of heart, deliverances from fear, inflowings of help, assurances of support."[2]

But at the heart of being Catholic is collective ritual. It may thrill our souls and excite our senses for a time and then feel oppressive at others. That is OK. The rituals of worship unite us, but they shouldn't leave us feeling tribal. Catholic rituals always reach out and beyond the practicing few; they lure and involve millions more than attend services regularly. Every ritual celebrates or reenacts the physical presence of Christ in some way. Many rituals originated—in their timing, elements, and even some of their language—in pagan traditions; but where pagan ceremonies focused on passing seasons and solstices, when these occasions were converted, they redeemed the earth through Christ's essential presence in it.

Ritual centers on sacraments, means for God to grace our lives in physical, tangible ways. There are seven sacraments by the official Catholic count. The first three—Baptism (cleansing water), Eucharist (nourishing bread), and Confirmation (growing up)—are called the sacraments of initiation.

The next two—Marriage and Holy Orders—reveal that not every sacrament is intended directly for every person. Not everyone is destined to marry, just as those who don't marry are not necessarily destined for Holy Orders (priesthood, deacon, monk, or nun). Nevertheless, vow-taking is for everyone, and marriage vows, as well as the solemn vow to a formal, religious life, are often similar to the sorts of vows one may make with Christ outside of marriage and monastery. This is why the symbolic language of "marriage" between us and God makes sense when we read it in the writings of the mystics or in the Song of Songs. This is also why monastic spirituality intrigues so many of us today, even though we may live domestic, married, lives.

The final two concern healing—the sort of healing that we all need at times: Reconciliation (penance and forgiveness) and Anointing the Sick. Penance and forgiveness is my favorite of all of them. As a Protestant, I was taught that only God forgives sins and that forgiveness is entirely between me and God. But as Chesterton once said, the first answer to the question of why he joined the Roman Catholic Church was "to get rid of my sins." He meant that the Catholic understands the reality of sin, first of all, and then the best way to abolish them: through confession and penance, which allow the brain and body to understand how forgiveness works: "The logic, which to many seems startling . . . , [is that] the Church deduces that sin confessed and adequately repented is actually abolished; and that the sinner does really begin again as if he had never sinned."[3]

The traditional sacraments are slowly coming back into vogue as Protestants and Catholics alike take new looks at old traditions. Christians are realizing that they need these rituals more than they need to understand *why* they need them. The sacraments offer regular opportunities for becoming spiritually healthy once again.

But it all begins with Baptism, the sacrament of initiation that involves us in faith for the first time. We were born to be baptized. In fact, in some ways, the water of birth is a sort of baptism. Our human bodies are curiously made so as to fight for life from the moment we are born, and yet we begin to die at the same time. Cells expire every second; new cells are born in their place.

There is a natural inclination within us to seek the water. "A wind from God swept over the face of the waters," it says in Genesis 1. Earth began as water, just as each of our lives begin in the water of our mother's womb. Water later destroyed the creation that God had called "good." In Judea in the early days of Jesus, his cousin, John, was baptizing people with water of repentance. When John baptized Jesus, it was at that moment that the Gospels first mention the Spirit of God that had appeared back in Genesis. The Spirit descended on Jesus like a dove.

Catholic spirituality has always begun in the waters of Baptism. In fact, Baptism is so central to Christian faith that it is one of the two or three most disputed tenets. Church people and theologians have bitterly argued over two millennia as to the proper form, the best age of the baptismal candidate, and whether or not to rebaptize someone who comes from one Christian tradition into another. (Catholics say emphatically no to this; once baptized is to be forever sealed as a child of God.)

The physical symbol of water represents the reality of the washing away of all that keeps us from God. According to the teachings of the Roman Catholic Church, it can actually be done privately, if and when necessary. In fact, it can even be administered by someone other than a priest—even by someone who does not understand or believe in its effectiveness—as long as the rite is performed correctly! God does the work of Baptism, not us.

But it is best to be baptized in church, among other people. Almost every religious ritual in every religious tradition is best practiced and understood together with others. Baptism is for us, but it is also for the gathered together. In Baptism, the priest says to the congregation, this child (or this adult) is one of yours. You are each to care for her and to see that she grows in knowledge and love of God.

Have your kids baptized in church. What they don't understand—what none of us really understands—grows inside us like seeds. Just as it is Catholic to emphasize the crucifix more than the Bible, it is Catholic to show our children what faith does before we try to explain to them what it means. Oscar Hijuelos portrays this beautifully in his novel *Mr. Ives' Christmas* between Mr. Ives and his young son, Robert:

> They would go off to church together, and the boy learned how to put his hands together in prayer, to kneel, to bow his head, and to make the Sign of the Cross. And Ives would tell him, "All this may seem confusing to

> you now, but when you're a little older it will become clear." He told him about how tongues of fire and soaring doves symbolized the spirit. He told him about the notion of a soul and guardian angels, and about the Holy Trinity.[4]

Choose sponsors or godparents. They will be the first among many in the congregation to see that the one baptized receives spiritual nurture. My favorite part of the Baptism ritual is what used to be commonly called the Exsufflation—a strange word that means "a blowing of breath to symbolize a sort of exorcism." This is when the priest breathes three times on the candidate, recalling the mysterious ways that Spirit (*Ruach* in Hebrew, which means "breath" or "wind") moves among us. Then the priest makes the sign of the cross with his thumb on the candidate's forehead and chest and says, "Receive the sign of the cross both upon your forehead + and also upon your heart +. Take to you the faith of the heavenly precepts; and so order your life as to be, from henceforth, the temple of God." Pronounced so simply, but the work of a lifetime.

Sacraments and Sacramentals

"Father Mackay," I said. "You know how Lord Marchmain greeted you last time you came; do you think it possible he can have changed now?"

"Thank God, by His grace it is possible."

"Perhaps," said Cara, "you could slip in while he is sleeping, say the words of absolution over him; he would never know."

The priest took the little silver box from his pocket and spoke again in Latin, touching the dying man with an oily wad; he finished what he had to do, put away the box and gave the final blessing. Suddenly Lord Marchmain moved his hand to his forehead; I thought he had felt the touch of the chrism and was wiping it away.

"O God," I prayed, "don't let him do that." But . . . the hand moved slowly down his breast, then to his shoulder, and Lord Marchmain made the sign of the cross.

—Evelyn Waugh, *Brideshead Revisited*[5]

There is scarcely any proper use of material things which cannot be directed toward the sanctification of men and the praise of God," explains the *Catechism of the Catholic Church* (1670). These material things are known as the sacramentals.

It is no wonder that Christians are often looking at the orthodox branches of other faiths for inspiration when it comes to spiritual practice. Orthodox religious traditions in Judaism and Islam often produce faithful practitioners in ways that put the average Christian to shame. We talk sometimes about the importance of the Sabbath, but the Orthodox Jew (and more and more, the Conservative and Reform Jew) actually keeps it sacred in ways that make them seem foolish to the rest of the world. We talk about praying continuously as Saint Paul urged, but the orthodox Muslim stops all that he's doing and rolls out his prayer mat five times a day. Five times daily, no matter where he finds himself, facing Mecca on a throw rug, bowing, prostrating, oblivious to whether or not I am standing nearby gawking at him. And then there are the kosher guidelines, the Sabbath customs, head coverings, and other rules about covering one's body that seem to infuse Orthodox and Hasidic Judaism, as well as traditional Muslim practices, with a powerful authenticity.

Jews and Muslims live secular lives with jobs and families and responsibilities, yet they often seem to manage to mark the hours and days with spiritual meaning in ways that pass Christians by. Many of us desire the sort of intense experiences of the presence of God in daily matters that we see others having. I have a modern Orthodox rabbi friend who, I know, has as many doubts about matters of faith as I have, and yet he pauses wherever we are about to have lunch and intones prayers in Hebrew. I envy him and his shamelessness.

It's not just that we respect them because they seem to follow principles that put themselves at odds with the dominant culture. We also admire them because they seem to live in a world that is constantly touching the Divine. We envy, at least, the tenacity with which they live with God.

For me, it has been the embarrassing faux pas more than earnestness that has thrust me into doing spiritual practices that I felt uncomfortable doing. There are times when *not doing* something is as inappropriate as *doing* the wrong thing. Some of my faux pas have come about because—and I know that this sounds crazy to those actually born Catholic—I have only recently become comfortable doing even the most basic of Catholic pieties.

I may have plenty of spiritual feeling and desire, but that doesn't mean I am comfortable doing religious practice. Growing up, we evangelical Protestants were taught not to do certain things: not to be charismatic, not to show piety in public, not to do anything by rote. I still feel self-conscious using the kneeler in front of me in church for fear that people will see that I'm putting on a show rather than going into my closet to pray. I still pray the Lord's Prayer with deliberate force in my words, not wanting my old pastors to hear that I might not be meaning every syllable I'm saying.

But as I said, a faux pas can be the quickest way to change behavior. I learned several years ago while not kneeling in church that not kneeling means that the people behind me will be kneeling directly into my upper back. It was the close breathing on the back of my neck that forced me finally to get off my rump and kneel as I was supposed to do!

Only in the last year have I been able to make the sign of the cross at the communion rail without feeling that my fundamentalist grandfathers are looking down at me with severe disapproval. I have met plenty of people like me in these things. Many converts and near-converts have difficulty getting religious practice to flow easily from religious feeling.

Spiritual practice is like exercise. That's how I look at it. The poet Gerard Manley Hopkins used to write down his sins in a notebook. Later, he would erase them from the pages, once they were confessed and hence forgiven.[6] The beauty of Catholic spirituality is the way in which we can use it. And that's where sacramentals come in.

There is a difference between a sacrament and a sacramental. The former is the means of grace formally instituted by Christ and the Church; the latter are the methods by which Catholics do their spiritual exercise. Sacramentals are all of the physical ways in which we make the occasions of life holy. These rites may change with time and circumstances, just as Saint Paul said they would back when he was writing to the church in Corinth. After advising the congregation on how to observe the sacrament of the Eucharist, or the Shared Meal, he finished by saying, "The other matters I shall arrange when I come" (1 Corinthians 11:34).

Sacramentals are by definition limitless. Many of the things discussed in Section Four were sacramentals: rosaries, little books, icons. There are many others, such as ashes (at Lent), bows and prostrations, vigil candles, holy water, incense, the sign of the cross, and chant. All of them have the power to spur on devotion, encouraging Catholics to express and deepen their love, sorrow, and joy. And almost every sacramental includes prayers. The *Catholic Encyclopedia* goes to great pains to explain that while sacraments certainly convey God's grace to us, "as experience teaches, the sacramentals do not infallibly produce their effect." Instead, sacramentals are more like private coaching from a Hall of Fame ball player to a rookie. These things work, he'll tell the new guy. Why wouldn't you try them?

An ancient Latin verse outlines the primary categories of sacramentals: *"Orans, tinctus, edens, confessus, dans, benedicens."* This roughly translates as "Public prayer, holy water, eating, confession, giving, and blessings."

Sometimes sacramentals change and in subtle ways cause spirituality to change. In the years before the Reformation, bells (a sacramental) were central to a sort of public Catholic piety in the cities of Europe. Church bells rang at the close of each workday, summoning the faithful to pray the Angelus and the De Profundis in honor to Our Lady, the Blessed Virgin Mary. This tradition was lost.

Recent changes in how Catholics receive the Eucharist at Mass are another example of sacramentals affecting spirituality. Since this sacrament is so important to practicing Catholic spirituality, changing sacramentals may have a wide and subtle effect on other aspects of faith. Catholics who used to kneel to receive and wait for the priest to place the communion host onto their tongue will now more often than not stand to receive it in their hands, placing the host on their tongue themselves. Some people have more trouble relating to the Real Presence of Christ if they are standing to receive it or touching it with their fingers.

Similarly, the reforms of the Second Vatican Council in the 1960s resulted in most churches removing the communion rails as people learned a new way to receive the sacrament. These changes seem superficial to the outside observer, but they have had a profound democratizing effect on many who experienced them; some have praised the changes, while others miss what was learned by kneeling, waiting, accepting. Sacramentals matter.

Contemplative Living

"Be still and know that I am God."

—God

"I think, therefore I am."

—Descartes

How many there must be who have smothered the first sparks of contemplation by piling wood on the fire before it was well lit.

—Thomas Merton, *Seeds of Contemplation*[7]

OK, God didn't necessarily say the first quote, but if we take Psalm 46 literally, God could have. Descartes certainly said the second one, and the third one speaks directly to people like me—who want it all, now, totally. Instead I've learned that contemplative living is a necessarily slow process, and it frames all of the rest of Catholic spiritual practice.

To use human thought as the fundamental stepping-stone for all other reality—as Descartes did—was the ultimate pinnacle of the Enlightenment. Unlike the Buddhist meaning of the term, the Enlightenment of the seventeenth and eighteenth centuries was a philosophical movement aimed at the separation of faith from reason. As in Descartes's "I think, therefore I am," not only is a Creator unnecessary for identity, but one's mind determines reality, rather than something outside of one's mind. Since the Enlightenment, we have been the ones giving meaning to ourselves.

Contemplative living flies in the face of this sort of thinking. The meaning of life is in contemplation, and contemplation is neither deep thinking nor science.

The Jesuits say it best. They use a triad to describe how faith encompasses the entire person: *Spiritu, corde, practice,* "In the spirit, from the heart, practically." Spirituality in the head alone is incomplete. A contemplative person lives and thinks and feels as one in communion with God and with others. A contemplative enjoys eternal things more than temporal ones, making decisions each day that reflect this, choosing to be quiet more often than noisy, becoming more and more comfortable in his or her skin and alone with God.

A contemplative person relates to God with his or her entire being. The most ordinary moments of daily activity can be filled with opportunities to learn these slower ways. For every moment that life is full, there should be other moments when it is blessedly empty. If this sounds a lot like how a monk or a nun must live, that's intentional. It is no accident that people are always discovering the virtues of monastic spirituality. For many, the monastery represents the only really authentic preserve of Christian spirituality today. When churches and clergy disappoint us, it seems that the monasteries carry on as they always have. In fact, monastics have carried on the contemplative life with the greatest success over the past two thousand years.

In many respects, we can all be monks. A contemplative life is for everyone, and to be like a monk is not necessarily to dress like one. To live as in a monastery is also possible, in some smaller measures, for everyone. Regardless of marriage, job, family, and other responsibilities, we can live in certain ways like monks and nuns. The silence of the monastery, for example (which terrifies many people at first), can become a kind of salvation. But essential to Catholic spirituality is the practice of silence; a contemplative approach to life is impossible without it.

One of the Desert Fathers, Abba Arsenius, loved to be alone and disliked the way that visitors from the cities would come out to see him, to seek him out. One day, some men arrived to ask Arsenius for wisdom. He said to them, "True solitude is like a young, pretty girl who is living in her father's house. Many young men come to see her, wishing for her hand in marriage. This young girl is attractive and desired by many, but no man really knows her. However, when she takes a husband, marries, and leaves her father's house, her life has changed forever. She is no longer adored by all. Some of the young men are probably very disappointed that she didn't choose them. Others forget about her altogether. She is no longer favored because her life is no longer hidden. The soul is this way also. When your soul is shown to everyone freely, it is no longer able to satisfy everyone."

The monastery is a place where believing rightly plays very little role in the day-to-day but where practice is central. The monastery may surprise you; on the outside, it appears to be a trap, a place that will strip away your freedom. But in truth, it is where people become free to be who they are meant to be. We live as in a monastery when we follow guidelines and rules that allow our real selves to come through and our false selves to fall away. Our false selves are those ways in which we perform for others or pretend to be what we are not.

The contemplative way of life is not focused on me. What I believe is not even in the top ten of what is most important. The contemplative life originates with and returns always to God. My hunger for silence, truth, honesty, and integrity are no accident. We are made for these things, even though we live in situations and often with goals that make achieving them nearly impossible. This hunger is best expressed by Thomas Kempis in his classic little book, *The Imitation of Christ.* Echoing Saint Augustine, who said that he could not rest except in God, Thomas writes, "You do not have here an abiding city; and wherever you may be, you are a stranger and pilgrim. You shall never rest until you are inwardly united with Christ."[8]

Even the way of believing is different for the contemplative person. It is a capacity to be developed, rather than a function of the brain. The contemplative is not satisfied to think and rationalize; he or she knows that there are more ways to understanding than thinking alone can find. To get behind thinking, or below it, is the goal of contemplatives, whether they are Zen, Sufi, Catholic, or Baptist. Think back to an occasion when you stopped analyzing a problem because you were frustrated in your attempts to solve it, only to realize a short while later that the solution seemed to present itself effortlessly to your mind. That is one way to get behind or below your thinking. The elimination of the problem is often the best solution to the problem. There is no on-off switch to the sort of believing that begins—or is rounded out by—contemplation.

The contemplative knows that the experience of transcendence—whether it comes from outside you or inside you—is true. And when people who have never had such experiences start to question them, the contemplative can offer no better explanation that to invite the doubters to come in. This is what the ancient Catholic tradition has done since the beginning: invited others to come and experience the goodness of knowing God. The contemplative Baron von Hugel once wrote, "I so love to watch cows as they browse at the borders, up against the hedges of fields. They move along, with their great tongues drawing in just only what they can assimilate; yes—but without stopping to snort defiantly against what does not thus suit them. . . . So ought we to do."[9]

But not all contemplative living is positive. Long silences, lengthy retreats, and a certain disposition lead some people to love a contemplative life perhaps a bit too much. More than once, I have spent time with a person who seemed to have spent too much time in meditation. The reactions slow and a certain mellowness takes root that almost borders on rot. We are all meant to be contemplatives, but not necessarily professional ones. I think the model of the monk in the world is the best approach.

As more Christians become contemplatives, organized faith has the potential to change and deepen. It is no accident that people in house churches, in Taize prayer groups, and other religious meetings outside of church buildings focus primarily on building contemplative lives. These movements may still revitalize the churches. The Anglican writer and mystic Evelyn Underhill said: "It is never the genuine mystic who talks about *dead forms*. He can reach out, through every religious form, to that Eternal Reality which it conveys. For him, every church will be a bridge-church, and all the various experiences of religion graded and partial revelations of the Being of Beings, the one full Reality—God."[10]

Eating and Kissing

Prayer and love are learned in the hour when prayer has become impossible and your heart has turned to stone.

—THOMAS MERTON, *SEEDS OF CONTEMPLATION*[11]

It is an old but true adage that we learn far more in a tempest than we do under blue skies. As Merton says, love may only become understandable in our lives once our hearts have hit rock bottom. And prayer becomes most real only when we have become completely word-weary.

In about the year 150, a man named Justin of Caesarea wrote a series of defenses of the fledgling Christian faith. He addressed himself to the rulers of the Roman Empire and to lovers of philosophy, saying that the persecution of Christians was wrong and that Christians represented the best of humans seeking to understand the meaning of existence. Justin was honored for his learning even in his own lifetime, but he was also martyred in Rome under the rule of Marcus Aurelius in about 165. He is known to posterity as Saint Justin the Martyr. Justin's *First Apology* offers the earliest and best explanation of what the first Christians did when they gathered together in worship:

> I will relate the manner in which we dedicated ourselves to God after we had been made new through Christ.
>
> As many as are persuaded and believe that what we teach and say is true, and undertake to be able to live accordingly . . . they are brought by us where there is water, and are regenerated in the same manner in which we were ourselves regenerated. For, in the name of God, the Father and Lord of the universe, and of our Savior Jesus Christ, and of the Holy Spirit, they then receive the washing with water.
>
> After we have washed him who has been convinced and has assented to our teaching, we bring him to the place where those who are called brethren are assembled, in order that we may offer hearty prayers in common. . . .
>
> Having ended the prayers, we salute one another with a kiss.
>
> There is then brought to the leader of the brethren bread and a cup of wine mixed with water; and he taking them, gives praise and glory to the Father of the universe, through the name of the Son and of the Holy Ghost, and offers thanks at considerable length for our being counted worthy to receive these things at His hands. And when he has concluded the prayers and thanksgivings, all the people present express their assent by saying "Amen."
>
> When the leader has given thanks, and all the people have expressed their assent, those who are called by us deacons give to each of those present to partake of the bread and wine mixed with water over which the thanksgiving was pronounced, and to those who are absent they carry away a portion.
>
> And this food is called by us the *Eucharist*, of which no one is allowed to partake but he who believes the

> things we teach are true, and who has been washed with the washing that is for the remission of sins, unto regeneration, and who is so living as Christ has enjoined. For not as common bread and common drink do we receive these; but as Jesus Christ our Savior, having been made flesh by the Word of God, had both flesh and blood for our salvation, so likewise have we been taught that the food which is blessed by the prayer of His word, and from which our blood and flesh by transmutation are nourished, is the flesh and blood of that Jesus who was made flesh.
>
> And the wealthy among us help the needy. And for all things with which we are supplied, we bless the Maker of all through His Son Jesus Christ, and through the Holy Ghost.
>
> On the day called Sunday, all who live in cities or in the country gather together to one place.
>
> If these things seem to you to be reasonable and true, honor them.[12]

The roots of all that happens in Catholic worship stems from Justin's sentences. Gathering together is central, even if it feels increasingly irrelevant today. And perhaps it is best summarized as eating and kissing.

Going or not going to services used to be the line of demarcation between being religious or just being spiritual. But virtual reality has changed all that. You can get religion, not just spirituality, on the Web. Electronic churches, synagogues, and mosques are everywhere. They feed the needs that people feel for spiritual connection to the Divine without the unpleasantness of having to actually leave one's house or be with other people. But although cyberfaith services can seem to be as authentic as physical-world services, they make a serious mistake by tricking people into the ancient fallacy or heresy that worship is something exclusively between you and God and that spirituality is primarily in your head or soul. You can't kiss a screen or eat a pixel.

There was a time, in my early twenties, when I left the organized church. I believed that walking in the woods and other contemplative experiences were real substitutes for getting together with others. I didn't realize just how Gnostic I was becoming. Gnosticism is best defined as salvation by knowledge, or spirituality of the mind. It is a heresy with ancient roots, and it is easy to fall into it accidentally.

Virtual services—using your computer to "enter" a sacred place and do religious things by pointing and clicking—are very un-Catholic in that they promote the idea that we are in control of our creation. The most Catholic thing you can do is to sit down beside strangers, friends, even people you dislike, to worship together. The physical presence of other bodies is what it is all about.

The physical presence of Christ is also what it is all about. There is nothing more central to Catholic faith than the Real Presence of Christ in the Eucharist. I believe in the Real Presence in the consecrated bread and wine of the Mass. I believe it because I choose to.

I crave mystery and am drawn to it even when it doesn't make sense to my brain. If our religious temperaments are determined for us in the first few years of life, mine was exceedingly cold and rational. We had evidences for faith, not mysteries. But what was for me a cold beam of rationality has turned into a love of mystery and spiritual practices that stems from it. Today, I'm almost like the character Sarah in Graham Greene's novel *The End of the Affair*. She says, "I believe the whole bag of tricks, there's nothing I don't believe, they could subdivide the Trinity into a dozen parts and I'd believe. They could dig up records that proved Christ had been invented by

Pilate to get himself promoted and I'd believe just the same. I've caught belief like a disease."[13]

It's not hard to believe in the Real Presence. On the contrary, I find it harder to believe that Christ might *not* be there. Divine presence is so common to me that it is easy to believe the whole package. As Nicholas of Cusa (1401–1464) once preached, "Christ is our bread [and] a spiritual food for our soul."[14] To believe this is to want it daily, as my Italian great-grandparents once did.

Eating his flesh and drinking his blood is strangely combined in the liturgy with forgiveness and the kiss of peace. We pray our confession, receive the assurance of forgiveness, and then turn to the people around us and kiss. Well, maybe we don't always kiss, but we at least shake hands! I have kissed those with whom I am arguing as well as those who have hurt me, and tears have come to my eyes. Maybe that's why we call it the kiss of peace and also why we talk about the blessings of obedience.

When I doubt God's existence or the meaning of the Eucharist or the value of gathering together with others to kiss and eat, I remember a passage from Chesterton's novel *The Ball and the Cross*. The scene features an outspoken atheist disputing religion with a young believer:

> "I do not love God. I do not want to find him; I do not think He is there to be found. . . . You are the happiest and most honest thing I ever saw in this godless universe. And I am the dirtiest and the most dishonest."
>
> Madeline looked at him doubtfully for an instant, and then said with a sudden simplicity and cheerfulness: "Oh, but if you are really sorry it is all right. If you are horribly sorry it is all the better. You have only to go and tell the priest so and he will give you God out of his own hands."

. . . "I am sure there is no God."

"But there is," said Madeline, quite quietly, and rather with the air of one telling children about an elephant. "Why I touched His body only this morning."

"You touched a bit of bread," said Turnbull, biting his knuckles. "Oh, I will say anything that can madden you."

"You think it is only a bit of bread," said the girl, and her lips tightened ever so little.

"I know it is only a bit of bread," said Turnbull, with violence.

She flung back her open face and smiled. "Then why do you refuse to eat it?"[15]

Millions of Blessings

Every baptized person is called to be a "blessing," and to bless.

—*Catechism of the Catholic Church* (1669)

Observant Jews are supposed to offer God one hundred blessings every day. I used to wonder what the purpose or meaning was in such blessings. Why would *humans* offer blessings to the Almighty? Why would our blessings matter? The answer is that blessings are not for the benefit of God; the purpose of blessings is to teach us to be thankful.

In Catholic spirituality, blessings take on a slightly different meaning. Moving beyond thankfulness, they are what we might call word-acts—occasions when words themselves have power. Consider those few times when you have said most genuinely, "I love you." Remember the first time that your teenage daughter (or you as a teenage daughter) said, "I hate you!" Not only do words such as these have power, but they are actions all by themselves. They create; we say these things because we believe that they will actually *create* love or hate.

Sometimes it is the painful situation that teaches this lesson most clearly. If you have ever gone for a long period of time telling your significant other that you love her and hearing the same words back in return, only to find out that your sweetheart didn't really mean it—you felt tremendous loss and grief. These emotions stem not from the incongruity of feeling between you and your partner but from the disparity of what actually existed in you and not in your partner.

So how does one human being bestow a "blessing" on another or on a thing? We sometimes say things that we believe makes something happen.

Most blessings are pronounced with other people present. Every blessing combines proclaiming the word of God, praising God's goodness, and asking for help. These are ways that we combine our intentions. A typical order of blessing will proceed something like this:

1. A brief spoken introduction stating why this person, situation, or thing requires blessing.
2. A simple rite, such as making the sign of the cross, and an introductory prayer, such as "The grace of our Lord Jesus Christ and the love of God and the fellowship of the Holy Spirit be with you all." And the others respond, "And also with you."
3. A short admonition on the inherent and related value of the person, situation, or thing.
4. Reading from scripture. Selected passages will emphasize themes such as the grace and goodness of God, God's wisdom and foundation for our lives, and how our help is always in the Lord.
5. A selected psalm. I like Psalm 121 for many occasional blessings:

> I lift up my eyes to the hills; from where is my help to come?
>
> My help comes from the LORD, the maker of heaven and earth.
>
> He will not let your foot be moved and he who watches over you will not fall asleep.
>
> Behold, he who keeps watch over Israel shall neither slumber nor sleep;
>
> The LORD himself watches over you; the LORD is your shade at your right hand,
>
> So that the sun shall not strike you by day, nor the moon by night.
>
> The LORD shall preserve you from all evil; it is he who shall keep you safe.
>
> The LORD shall watch over your going out and your coming in, from this time forth for evermore.

6. An actual prayer of blessing. "Lord Jesus Christ, we bless this . . ."
7. A conclusion that summarizes the action of what is happening in and through the blessing. "May the Lord almighty bless you and receive the desires of your hearts." "May the Lord give you trust in him, so that you will do all things in his name." "May the Lord watch over you and give you peace." Each conclusion is followed by "Amen" from everyone gathered together. And that's the best part.

According to the official Roman Catholic *Book of Blessings*, we run the gamut of subjects alphabetically from "Addictions" and "Adopted Children" to "Wine" and "Work Tools and Equipment," with plenty of subjects in between. My favorites are blessings for things we normally don't see as blessable: boats, chairs, elderly people confined to their homes, even mouths and feet. I also say blessings over my children—even now that they are teenagers and find the practice occasionally embarrassing!

A blessing also contains a promise of Divine help, a confidence in God's presence, and a reassurance that God will be with us. To bless another is to give the recipient meaning and holiness, to connect human and Divine intentions, and to declare hope for something more than what is easily seen. The Torah says that Yahweh asked Moses to tell the priests to learn to say over the people:

> The Lord bless you and keep you;
> The Lord make his face to shine upon you, and be gracious to you;
> The Lord lift up his countenance upon you, and give you peace [Numbers 6:24–26].

The full meaning of blessings is that we all can create Divine presence, and occasionally, we pronounce it out loud. We might want to take the old priestly blessing and make our lives into blessings, like this:

> Bless each other and keep each other;
> Make your face to shine upon each other, and be gracious to one another;
> As the Lord lifts up his countenance upon you, and gives you peace, do likewise wherever you go.

Catholics are supposed to bless everything under the sun with word and action. Francis of Assisi once said, "Preach Christ crucified, and when necessary, use words." In other words, become a living expression of Christ in your daily life, but then sometimes, use words to pronounce and make it real in another way.

Excommunication

We need the Church. The Church could very easily do without us.

—JEFFREY SMITH, "ROVING MEDIEVALIST"[16]

To be excommunicated means to literally be "out of communion." Paul wrote to the church at Corinth, "If there is anyone who does not love the Lord, a curse on such a one" (1 Corinthians 16:22). He wasn't messing around. The new communities of Christians were fighting for their lives, and they had almost a military mentality regarding loyalty. In that same spirit, the Catholic Church has excommunicated many people over the centuries when it felt most embattled:

- The Franciscan philosopher William of Ockham in 1328 for calling Pope John XII a heretic
- The Czech reformer Jan Hus in 1411
- The German reformer Martin Luther in 1521
- England's King Henry VIII in 1533 for many accumulated offenses: declaring himself the head of the

Church in England, destroying and disbursing the monasteries in England, and desecrating shrines, including that of Saint Thomas Becket at Canterbury

The politics in these cases were clear. Cutting ties with someone who has already broken ties with you makes sense. I can also understand why a church might need to officially denounce certain people, such as Edwin González Concepción, a firefighter in Puerto Rico, who recently claimed that Pope Benedict XVI is the Antichrist and that he, Concepción, is the reincarnation of Pope John Paul II. Other uses of declaring someone "accursed," however, are simply motivated by fear or greed. One or both of these motivations led to the condemnation and excommunication of any Catholic involved in a secret society (the Freemasons) back in 1738. Even Pope Clement XII's statement of excommunication sounded fearful and unsure of itself: "Under an outward semblance of natural probity, which they require, and which they regard as sufficient they [the Freemasons] have established certain laws and statutes binding themselves towards each other ... but since crime ultimately betrays itself ... their assemblies have become to the faithful such objects of suspicion that every good man now regards affiliation to them as a certain indication of wickedness and perversion."

Other explicitly political uses of excommunication have been more subtle—and less excusable. There was the priest in Nebraska who was excommunicated in 1901 for publicly declaring his sympathy for the cause of Protestants in Ireland, and many Catholics have been excommunicated by their bishops or popes for being on the wrong side in a war, such as Pope Leo XII's condemning of any Catholic who opposed the monarchies of Spain and Portugal in the nineteenth century.

It stands to reason that the same argument that makes capital punishment always wrong should make excommunication always wrong. No one should be able to deny another person the right to be in communion with Christ. In truth, no one can. Excommunication only sets one outside the Church, or at least outside the sacraments of the Church. It is not comparable to a death penalty because no one can ever take away your Baptism. Excommunication is more comparable to torture than death. Whether for apostasy, heresy, schism, desecration of the Eucharist, or being an accomplice to any of these unseemly things, the Church says that excommunication is good medicine and that its purpose is to force you back to repentance—and to the sacrament of forgiveness.

I'll never be in a position to give apostasy or heresy much consideration, but I do wonder if excommunication might be exactly what some people need. In fact, in a lot of respects, we all need to be kicked out. Then we may be able to see more clearly what it means to be Catholic. You can be so close that you do not see. Even as I envy the habits of devotion that often characterize the cradle Catholic, I can also see how being almost Catholic may even be preferable.

Pierre Teilhard de Chardin, the French paleontologist and Jesuit priest of the twentieth century who once said he wished to be "hyper-Catholic" (see "Sacred Spaces and Places" in Section Two), also experienced his greatest religious insight when he was far from the familiar cathedrals of his youth. Teilhard was in the middle of an expedition in the desert of Ordos in remote China, near the border with Mongolia, when he discovered that he had no elements of bread and wine (what Catholics call "physical signs") with which to celebrate the Holy Eucharist. Physical signs are essential for sacraments. You can't just imagine the process or conjure it in your mind. Teilhard's meditation, written on the morning of the Feast of the Transfiguration, was thirty-six pages long and came to be published only after his death decades later. It is called "The Mass on the World."[17]

At first unable to offer the Mass as he had been taught to do, Teilhard reconsidered its meaning, meditating on the essential presence of Christ in the universe in all of its elements. His sacrificial offering that morning extended the eucharistic experience to all matter. When the priest recites "This is my body . . ." and "This is my blood . . ." in the eucharistic prayer, Teilhard gave these words the cosmic meaning that Jesus must have intended. The sacrifice of Christ spreads across all matter in the universe, just as the Incarnation of Christ did. All matter is consecrated by the host, which is the Divine Word; all matter is atoned in the wine. He is echoing Saint Paul more than the account of the Last Supper in the Gospels:

> Blessed be God the Father. . . . He has let us know the mystery of his purpose, according to his good pleasure which he determined beforehand in Christ, for him to act upon when the times had run their course: that he would bring everything together under Christ, as head, everything in the heavens and everything on earth [Ephesians 1:3a, 9–10].

We might say the same for all Christians, both Catholic and not—"that he would bring everything together under Christ." Without diminishing the importance of the elements of bread and wine, Teilhard showed how the message can become fenced in, insulated, when our imaginations are limited to what we have always done. Teilhard's eucharistic vision flattens the world and puts God in the middle, like a magnet. On that Feast of the Transfiguration, without elements of bread and wine, all matter became, through the Incarnation,

Crucifixion, and Resurrection, the body and blood of Christ. The physical symbols of bread and wine bring the Real Presence of Christ into our bodies in tangible ways (we eat them), but the true host was the universe made flesh. All of matter was God incarnate.

Conversion can mean to change or translate, as one would convert difficult directions into more readily understandable ones. Or conversion may mean to switch or transfer, as one might convert from a northbound train to a southbound one. It is this second sort of conversion—the meaning that involves turning completely around—that seems increasingly irrelevant to me. Conversion happens. Whether you like it or not, conversion happens. Life comes into sharper focus. The false self fades away, and the true self begins to emerge. The meaning of life blossoms before our eyes. Our values change; our imagination is kindled, for what is and for what is possible. Our vocation is set before us, and God is speaking within us. Catholic spirituality is ultimately about being increasingly at home in what at first seems somewhat alien to us. All of the history, practice, and mystery point toward this one thing: to be possessed, and to love it.

APPENDIX

Defining a Few Terms

ashes A symbol of penance, primarily used in church on Ash Wednesday when the priest applies them in the sign of the cross to your forehead to remind you of your mortality and your reliance on God's grace.

apostolic succession The unbroken chain of religious authority that connects the original apostles with bishops today. A new bishop is always consecrated into the role by one or more current bishops through the "laying on of hands," which physically symbolizes this succession.

Ascension A feast, or formal celebration, in the Roman Catholic Church, remembering the original occasion when Christ rose to heaven after the Resurrection.

Book of Blessings An official publication of the Roman Catholic Church, first published in 1984, intended to reflect the principles elucidated at the Second Vatican Council regarding the blessings available for all things, places, and people.

Book of Hours A prayer book, often commissioned by a wealthy patron and originally produced only in monasteries, containing lavish illustrations and beautiful calligraphy.

breviary A book or series of books used by monks, nuns, and many nonmonastics to pray the daily Liturgy of the Hours.

canonization A formal declaration from the pope that a deceased person is a saint and that veneration of that person is efficacious for all Christians. In making this declaration, the pope attests to the holiness of the candidate's life and authenticates at least two miracles performed through the person's intercession.

chrism Oil blessed for the purpose of applying to the foreheads of people at Baptism, Confirmation, and other special occasions. *Chrism,* like *Christ,* comes from a Greek word meaning "anointing."

communion of saints All the faithful, both departed and on earth, held by grace in one community as the children of God. Without reference to canonization, all the faithful departed are saints who urge on those of us who are still living, and we who are alive pray to them for spiritual intercession and prayer.

diocese A geographic region of the church headed by a bishop.

ecumenical Encompassing all rites and expressions of the Catholic Church.

feast day A day set aside each year for liturgically honoring a saint. A saint's feast day is usually the day of his or her death, which is also the day of his or her new eternal life.

iconoclasm The practice of destroying religious images and removing them from churches and devotional life, as ordered and sanctioned by both secular and religious leaders in the eighth, ninth, and sixteenth centuries.

lectio divina Latin for "Divine reading"; a popular spiritual practice inspired by monastic spirituality that combines prayer and reading, listening for God's voice while taking in the words and ideas on the page.

marginalia Notes and doodles jotted in the margins of a book while responding to and interacting with the material rather than passively reading it. The term was coined by the Romantic poet and spiritual thinker Samuel Taylor Coleridge.

Mariology The study and teaching of the doctrines of the Blessed Virgin Mary. The adjective *Marian* is used to describe the Virgin's qualities, features, and influences.

Nicene Creed One of the two most important creeds (summaries of the tenets of faith) in the Roman Catholic Church; this one was composed as the result of two ecumenical gatherings of theologians in 325 (at Nicaea) and 381 (at Constantinople).

novenas Petitionary prayers offered to God on special occasions, repeated over nine consecutive days, asking for Divine guidance or intercession.

Sacred Heart of Jesus The human heart of Jesus Christ, often pictured in popular devotion as enlarged and superimposed on images of the Savior. The phrase also refers equally to the qualities of his heart: gentle, unsurpassing love.

Second Vatican Council The most important ecumenical council since late antiquity. Originally convened by Pope John XXIII in 1962, Vatican II, as it is often called, resulted in dramatic liturgical reforms, new roles for the laity in worship and religious life, greater outreach to the poor, and openness to people of other Christian denominations and other faiths.

Taize An ecumenical Christian community formed in 1940 in France. About one hundred men of various Protestant and Roman Catholic backgrounds live there, but the community is primarily known as a place of pilgrimage and retreat, visited by thousands of young people each year. The term also refers to the simple chant style of meditation and worship that originated in this community.

Torah The most important scriptures in Judaism, also known as the Five Books of Moses, constituting the first five books of the Hebrew Bible (the Old Testament). The word *Torah* means "teaching" or "law" in Hebrew.

Zohar The most foundational and classical text of Jewish spirituality or kabbalah, composed in Spain probably in the thirteenth century.

NOTES

INTRODUCTION

1. Thomas Howard, *Lead, Kindly Light: My Journey to Rome* (San Francisco: Ignatius Press, 2004), p. 88.

SECTION ONE: THE LANGUAGE AND THE SPIRIT

1. Flannery O'Connor, "Letter to Louise Abbot" (1959), in Sally Fitzgerald (ed.), *The Habit of Being: Letters of Flannery O'Connor* (New York: Farrar, Straus & Giroux, 1988), p. 354.
2. Joseph Ratzinger, Pope Benedict XVI, *Jesus of Nazareth: From the Baptism in the Jordan to the Transfiguration* (New York: Doubleday, 2007), pp. xxiii–xxiv.
3. Dean H. Hamer, *The God Gene: How Faith Is Hardwired into Our Genes* (New York: Anchor Books, 2005).
4. Graham Greene, *A Burnt-Out Case* (New York: Penguin Classics, 1992), p. 124. (Originally published 1961.)
5. Richard Dawkins, *The God Delusion* (Boston: Houghton Mifflin, 2006).
6. Marilynne Robinson, "Onward, Christian Liberals," *American Scholar,* Spring 2006, p. 43.
7. Mary Gordon, "Temporary Shelter," in *The Stories of Mary Gordon* (New York: Pantheon Books, 2006), p. 278.

8. G. K. Chesterton, *The Ball and the Cross* (Whitefish, Mont.: Kessenger, 2004), p. 43. (Originally published 1910.)
9. Thomas Howard, *Lead, Kindly Light: My Journey to Rome* (San Francisco: Ignatius Press, 2004), p. 27.
10. Martin Luther, quoted in Joseph Leo Koerner, *The Reformation of the Image* (Chicago: University of Chicago Press, 2004), p. 201.
11. Scott Cairns, *Love's Immensity: Mystics on the Endless Life* (Brewster, Mass.: Paraclete Press, 2007), p. 7.
12. Léon Bloy, *The Woman Who Was Poor*, trans. I. J. Collins (New York: Sheed & Ward, 1947), pp. 251–252. (Originally published 1897.)
13. William Blake, "London" (1820).
14. Henry Adams, *Mont-Saint-Michel and Chartres* (New York: Penguin, 1986), p. 359. (Originally published 1913.)
15. Brian McLaren, *A Generous Orthodoxy* (Grand Rapids, Mich.: Zondervan, 2004), p. 199.
16. Malcolm Muggeridge, "How Does One Find Faith?" Interview with William F. Buckley Jr., *Firing Line,* Public Broadcasting System, Oct. 5, 1980.
17. George Bernard Shaw, *Saint Joan* (1923), in Philip G. Hill (ed.), *Our Dramatic Heritage,* Vol. 5: *Reactions to Realism* (Rutherford, N.J.: Fairleigh Dickinson University Press, 1991), p. 88.
18. Murray Roston, *Graham Greene's Narrative Strategies: A Study of the Major Novels* (New York: Palgrave Macmillan, 2006), p. 4.
19. John Humphrys, *In God We Doubt: Confessions of an Angry Agnostic* (London: Hodder & Stoughton, 2007).
20. Shaw, *Saint Joan,* in Hill, *Our Dramatic Heritage,* p. 137.
21. Quoted in E. Stanley Jones, *The Christ of the Indian Road* (New York: Abingdon Press, 1925), p. 78. C. F. Andrews, an Anglican missionary to India, also compared Gandhi to Saint Francis in several places in his books, including *Mahatma Gandhi's Ideas Including Selections from His Writings* (London: Allen & Unwin, 1929).

22. Evelyn Waugh, *Brideshead Revisited* (New York: Back Bay, 1999), p. 192. (Originally published 1945.)

SECTION TWO: THE CATHOLIC IMAGINATION

1. Shaw, *Saint Joan,* in Hill, *Our Dramatic Heritage,* p. 89.
2. Flannery O'Connor, "The Fiction Writer and His Country," in *Collected Works* (New York: Library of America, 1988), p. 860.
3. Miguel de Unamuno, *Our Lord Don Quixote,* trans. Anthony Kerrigan (Princeton, N.J.: Princeton University Press, 1967), p. 11. (Originally published 1905.)
4. All quotes from scripture are from *The Jerusalem Bible* unless otherwise noted.
5. *The Age of Bede,* trans. J. F. Webb, ed. David Farmer (Harmondsworth, England: Penguin, 1965), p. 213.
6. James Joyce, *A Portrait of the Artist as a Young Man* (New York: Viking Press, 1958), p. 232.
7. From a letter, quoted in Robert Speaight, *Teilhard de Chardin: A Biography* (London: Collins, 1967), p. 171.
8. Robert A. Scott, *The Gothic Enterprise: A Guide to Understanding the Medieval Cathedral* (Berkeley: University of California Press, 2003), pp. 17–18, 131–132.
9. Raïssa Maritain, *We Have Been Friends Together,* trans. Julie Kernan (New York: Longmans, Green, 1942), p. 150.
10. My own translation; for comparison, see M. O. Walshe (ed. and trans.), *Meister Eckhart: Sermons and Treatises,* Vol. 1 (Dorset, England: Element Books, 1987), p. 1.
11. Waugh, *Brideshead Revisited,* p. 86.
12. Oscar Hijuelos, *Mr. Ives' Christmas* (New York: HarperPerennial, 1996), pp. 100–102.
13. Thomas Merton, *Conjectures of a Guilty Bystander* (Garden City, N.Y.: Doubleday, 1966), pp. 140–141.
14. *Bernard of Clairvaux: The Parables and the Sentences,* trans. Michael Casey, ed. Maureen M. O'Brien (Kalamazoo, Mich.: Cistercian, 2000), pp. 119–120.

15. William Blake, "Milton" (1808).
16. William Blake, "Jerusalem" (1820).
17. Graham Greene, interview with John Cornwell, *The Tablet,* Sept. 1989.
18. Graham Greene, *Monsieur Quixote* (London: Bodley Head, 1982), p. 139.
19. Cyril of Jerusalem, *Catecheses,* 26, 28; translation of the *Catholic Encyclopedia* with slight modifications.
20. Czeslaw Milosz, *Visions from San Francisco Bay,* trans. Richard Lourie (New York: Farrar, Straus & Giroux, 1982), p. 33.
21. John Henry Cardinal Newman, *Apologia Pro Vita Sua,* pt. vii.
22. Ibid.
23. This online resource is a boon to learning about Catholicism. Many of the articles are decades old, but most have also been slightly updated in recent years. Visit http://www.newadvent.org/cathen/index.html.
24. Theo Hobson, "The Church That Lost Its Spirit," *London Times,* May 7, 2005.
25. Jacques Maritain, *Three Reformers* (Westport, Conn.: Greenwood Press, 1970), p. 14. (Originally published 1928.)
26. This is my own translation.
27. Czeslaw Milosz, *Legends of Modernity: Essays and Letters from Occupied Poland, 1942–1943,* trans. Madeline G. Levine (New York: Farrar, Straus & Giroux, 2005), p. 211.
28. Howard, *Lead, Kindly Light,* p. 40.
29. Pierre Teilhard de Chardin, *Hymn of the Universe* (New York: HarperCollins, 1961), p. 26.
30. Ibid., p. 31.

SECTION THREE: FAITH WITH FLESH

1. Brother Lawrence, *The Practice of the Presence of God,* trans. Robert J. Edmonson (Brewster, Mass.: Paraclete Press, 1985), p. 72.
2. Walter Percy, *Love in the Ruins: The Adventures of a Bad Catholic at a Time near the End of the World* (New York: Picador USA, 1999), p. 254. (Originally published 1971.)

3. Samuel Taylor Coleridge, *Aids to Reflection* (1825).
4. Douglas G. Brinkley (ed.), *Windblown World: The Journals of Jack Kerouac, 1947–1954* (New York: Penguin, 2006), p. 177.
5. O'Connor, "Fiction Writer and His Country," p. 855.
6. I thank Peter Rollins, the Belfast philosopher and founder of Ikon, for these insights about Saint Anselm.
7. C. S. Lewis, *An Experiment in Criticism* (New York: Cambridge University Press, 1961), p. 17.
8. G. K. Chesterton, *The Autobiography of G. K. Chesterton* (New York: Sheed & Ward, 1936), p. 249.
9. D. H. Lawrence, *The Rainbow* (New York: Huebsch, 1921), p. 265.
10. Simone Weil, *Letter to a Priest,* trans. Arthur Wills (New York: Putnam, 1954), pp. 34–35.
11. David Warren, "Consumer's Guide," *Crisis,* April 2007, p. 10.
12. Waugh, *Brideshead Revisited,* p. 86.
13. Muriel Spark, *Memento Mori* (New York: New Directions, 2000), p. 153. (Originally published 1959.)
14. Tertullian, *The Apology of Tertullian,* trans. T. H. Bindley (Oxford: Parker, 1890), ch. 33.
15. John Milton, *Paradise Lost,* bk. 1.
16. Cardinal Joseph Ratzinger, *Eschatology: Death and Eternal Life* (Washington, D.C.: Catholic University of America Press, 1988), p. 68.
17. Dorothy Sayers, *The Divine Comedy.* Vol. 1: *Hell* (Harmondsworth, England: Penguin Books, 1951), p. 11.
18. Eamon Duffy, *Faith of Our Fathers: Reflections on Catholic Traditions* (New York: Continuum, 2006), p. 44.
19. John Donne, "Good Friday, 1613," ll. 36–42.

SECTION FOUR: MUCH MORE THAN KITSCH AND JESUS JUNK

1. Gary Wills, *The Rosary: Prayer Comes Round* (New York: Penguin, 2006), p. 1.
2. D. H. Lawrence, *Apocalypse* (New York: Penguin, 1976), p. 3.
3. Lawrence S. Cunningham, "Catholic Spirituality: What Does It Mean Today?" *Commonweal,* Feb. 24, 2006, p. 11.

4. Richard Crashaw, "On a Prayer Book Sent to Mrs. M. R.," ll. 17–20. I have modernized the spellings.
5. John Osborne, *Luther,* in *Plays Three* (Boston: Faber & Faber, 1998), p. 40.
6. Trevor Cooper (ed.), *The Journal of William Dowsing: Iconoclasm in East Anglia During the English Civil War* (Woodbridge, England: Boydell Press, 2001), p. 214.
7. Quoted in Robert Maniura, *Pilgrimage to Images in the Fifteenth Century: The Origins of the Cult of Our Lady of Czestochowa* (Woodbridge, England: Boydell Press, 2004), p. 133.
8. Jim Forest, *Praying with Icons* (Maryknoll, N.Y.: Orbis, 1997), p. 45.
9. Graham Greene, *The Heart of the Matter* (New York: Penguin, 1999), p. 242. (Originally published 1948.)
10. Shaw, *Saint Joan,* preface.
11. This first quotation from Psalms is from the NRSV version. All others are from the Book of Common Prayer.
12. Rev. Father Andrew, S.D.C., *Meditations for Every Day* (New York: Morehouse-Barlow, 1934), p. 143.
13. Herman Melville, *Redburn: His First Voyage,* in *Herman Melville: Redburn, White-Jacket, Moby-Dick* (Washington, D.C.: Library of America, 1983), p. 148. (Originally published 1850.)
14. Chesterton, *Autobiography,* pp. 340–341.
15. Gerard Manley Hopkins, letter to Robert Bridges, Oct. 24, 1883.
16. Eamon Duffy, "Confessions of a Cradle Catholic," *Pastoral Review,* Jan. 2000, p. 14.
17. William Butler Yeats, *The Collected Letters of W. B. Yeats,* Vol. 1, ed. John Kelly (Oxford: Clarendon Press, 1986), p. 8.
18. Thomas Kempis, *The Imitation of Christ,* bk. 2, ch. 1. My translation.

SECTION FIVE: MY OWN CLOUD OF WITNESSES

1. Paul Sabatier, *The Road to Assisi: The Essential Biography of St. Francis,* ed. Jon M. Sweeney (Brewster, Mass.: Paraclete Press, 2004), p. 81. (Originally published 1894.)

2. John Wesley, quoted in David Sloan Wilson, *Evolution for Everyone: How Darwin's Theory Can Change the Way We Think About Our Lives* (New York: Delacourte Press, 2007), p. 248.
3. Didache, 16.1.
4. Douglas Brinkley (ed.), *Windblown World* (New York: Penguin, 2006), pp. xxii–xxiii.
5. Ibid., pp. 15, 158.
6. Charles de Foucauld, *Writings,* ed. Robert Ellsberg (Maryknoll, N.Y.: Orbis Books, 2003), p. 124.
7. G. Janouch, *Conversations with Kafka* (London: Secker & Warburg, 1953), p. 57.
8. Maisie Ward, *Return to Chesterton* (New York: Sheed & Ward, 1952), p. 7.
9. Anne Enright, "Diary," *London Review of Books,* May 10, 2007, p. 43.
10. Chesterton, *Autobiography,* p. 189.
11. G. K. Chesterton, "The Hammer of God," in *The Innocence of Father Brown* (Rockville, Md.: Wildside Press, 2004), p. 170. (Originally published 1911.)
12. G. K. Chesterton, *Orthodoxy: The Romance of Faith* (Fort Collins, Colo.: Ignatius Press, 1995), p. 108. (Originally published 1908.)
13. Flannery O'Connor, "Fiction Writer and His Country," pp. 805–806.
14. Ibid., p. 805.
15. Quoted in Jorge Luis Borges, "On the Cult of Books," in *Selected Non-Fictions* (New York: Viking Press, 1999), pp. 361–362. (Originally published in 1912.)

SECTION SIX: TOGETHER WITH OTHERS

1. Howard, *Lead, Kindly Light,* p. 89.
2. I know of no better summary than this one, by William James. Quoted in Robert D. Richardson, *William James: In the Maelstrom of American Modernism* (Boston: Houghton Mifflin, 2006), p. 379.

3. Chesterton, *Autobiography,* pp. 340, 353.
4. Hijuelos, *Mr. Ives' Christmas,* pp. 72–73.
5. Waugh, *Brideshead Revisited,* p. 338.
6. W. H. Gardner, *Gerard Manley Hopkins: A Study of Poetic Idiosyncrasy in Relation to Poetic Tradition,* Vol. 1 (New York: Oxford University Press, 1958), p. 5.
7. Thomas Merton, "Detachment," in *Seeds of Contemplation* (New York: New Directions, 1949), p. 128.
8. Kempis, *The Imitation of Christ,* bk. 2, ch. 1. My translation.
9. Baron F. von Hugel, quoted in Evelyn Underhill, *Mixed Pasture: Twelve Essays and Addresses* (New York: Longmans, Green, 1933), p. xii.
10. Underhill, *Mixed Pasture,* p. 21.
11. Thomas Merton, "Distractions," in *Seeds of Contemplation,* p. 140.
12. Saint Justin the Martyr, *First Apology,* chs. 61, 65–68. This translation is adapted slightly from the one available at the *Catholic Encyclopedia* online.
13. Graham Greene, *The End of the Affair* (New York: Penguin Books, 1999), pp. 146–147. (Originally published 1951.)
14. Quoted in Ann W. Astell, *Eating Beauty: The Eucharist and the Spiritual Arts of the Middle Ages* (Ithaca, N.Y.: Cornell University Press, 2006), p. 2.
15. Chesterton, *Ball and the Cross,* pp. 113–115.
16. Jeffrey Smith, "Roving Medievalist" (blog), http://www.rovingmedievalist.blogspot.com. Accessed on June 1, 2007.
17. Pierre Teilhard de Chardin, "The Mass on the World," in *Hymn of the Universe,* pp. 11–12.

ACKNOWLEDGMENTS

1. Barbara Kingsolver, "The Art of Buying Nothing," in *Wendell Berry: Life and Work,* ed. by Jason Peters (Lexington: The University Press of Kentucky, 2007), p. 294.

SUGGESTIONS FOR FURTHER READING

A Catholic writer will not always produce a Catholic book. J.R.R. Tolkein's *Lord of the Rings,* for instance, would never be called "Catholic" except in the broadest sense (which reduces the meaning to just about nothing). Here is a sampling of what I regard to be some of the most important nontheological Catholic books published over the centuries. Each of them reveals in profound ways one or more aspects of the Catholic imagination. They are works of spirituality, hagiography, memoir or biography, and fiction. I've listed them in chronological order.

Saint Augustine of Hippo, *Confessions.* Written in 397–398. Still in print.

Jacobus de Voragine, *The Golden Legend* (hagiography/spirituality). Compiled in the thirteenth century. Still in print.

Author unknown, *The Little Flowers of Saint Francis* (memoir/biography). First written and circulated in the fourteenth century. Still in print.

Thomas Kempis, *The Imitation of Christ* (spirituality). Written in the 1420s. Still in print.

Saint Teresa of Avila, *Autobiography* (memoir/autobiography). Written in the 1560s. Also sometimes called *The Life of St. Teresa of Jesus.* Still in print.

Brother Lawrence, *The Practice of the Presence of God* (spirituality). First published after his death in 1691. Still in print.

Saint Thérèse of Lisieux, *The Story of a Soul* (memoir/autobiography). Written in 1895–1897 and published after her death. Still in print.

Léon Bloy, *The Woman Who Was Poor* (novel). Published in French in 1897 and in English in 1947. Currently out of print.

G. K. Chesterton, *Orthodoxy: The Romance of Faith* (spirituality). Published in 1908. Still in print.

G. K. Chesterton, *Saint Francis* (spirituality). Published in 1923. Still in print.

Evelyn Waugh, *Brideshead Revisited* (novel). Published in 1945. Still in print.

Thomas Merton, *The Seven Storey Mountain* (memoir/autobiography). New York: Harvest Books, 1999. First published in 1948.

Flannery O'Connor, *A Good Man Is Hard to Find*, *Wise Blood*, and *Mystery and Manners* (stories, novel, letters—in 1955, 1962, and 1969). These are now all available together, plus more material, in *Collected Works.* New York: Library of America, 1988.

Graham Greene, *Monsignor Quixote* (novel). London: Bodley Head, 1982. Currently out of print.

Oscar Hijuelos, *Mr. Ives' Christmas* (novel). New York: HarperPerennial, 1996.

ACKNOWLEDGMENTS

The novelist Barbara Kingsolver recently wrote, "To save my life I can't write a book from beginning to end. I seem to write them from the inside out, twisting them around like a dog trying to put on a pair of pajamas, panting and craning my neck until I've finally gotten the thing buttoned up, face-forward, right side out."[1] I have the same problem, and nowhere more acutely than in the book you are holding now. In whatever measure I have succeeded in getting my thoughts right side out, I probably owe most of the thanks to my editor at Jossey-Bass, Sheryl Fullerton.

Thanks also to the many friends who have discussed these ideas with me over the last few years. I'm thinking in particular of Pat-Marie Hawkinson; Brendan Walsh; Maura Shaw; the Rev. Christina Brannock-Wanter; the late M. Basil Pennington, OCSO; Rabbi Phil Miller; Rabbi Lawrence Kushner; Carol Showalter; Peter Rollins; Donald Wells; Steve Swayne; and Father Matt Torpley, OCSO.

J.M.S.

THE AUTHOR

Jon M. Sweeney is a writer, editor, retreat leader, and popular speaker. He is best known as the author of books that present key people, events, and legends of the Middle Ages to a wide audience. His book *Light in the Dark Ages: The Friendship of Francis and Clare of Assisi,* was a selection of Crossings Book Club, the History Book Club, and the Book-of-the-Month Club, as well as the One Spirit, Reader's Subscription, and Quality Paperback book clubs.

For many years, Sweeney was the editor in chief of SkyLight Paths Publishing, a multifaith trade book publisher in Vermont that he cofounded. Since 2004, he has been the associate publisher at Paraclete Press in Massachusetts.

In addition to writing for the popular Explorefaith.org Web site, Sweeney writes for magazines including *Catholic Digest* and *The Lutheran.* He is one of the contributors to the popular daily devotional, *Daily Guideposts 2008.* He is an Episcopalian. He worships at Saint James' Episcopal Church in Woodstock, Vermont, and was appointed by his bishop in 2006 to the Committee on Discernment for the diocese of Vermont.

He is a frequent guest speaker to groups of all denominational backgrounds on the subjects of understanding the Virgin Mary, Francis and Clare of Assisi and Franciscan spirituality, and appreciating the Catholic imagination. He was the featured speaker at the National Cathedral in Washington, D.C., on the feast day of Saint Francis in 2004.

Sweeney lives in Vermont. Visit Jon's "Almost Catholic" blog at www.jonmsweeney.wordpress.com.